The (Im)Possible Beekeeper

Commonsense methods of making beekeeping fun and functional once again

Caroline Abbott

Illustrations and Graphic Design by

Elizabeth Abbott

A special thank you to all my friends and fellow beekeepers who have encouraged me to share this information with a wider audience.

Introduction

This book was born from a sense of frustration and a desire to restore something that seemed lost to me. I began my beekeeping journey in 2005. It was at a time when many beekeepers felt they were getting a bit of an upper hand on the varroa mite and in fact many beekeepers who had left beekeeping in frustration in the late 1980's were giving it a go once again. Many of the beekeepers in my local club were aging out. At age 40 I was the youngest person in the club besides my 13 year old daughter who came with me to meetings. Both my daughter and I were readers and had studied many of the older beekeeping books. We found that at meetings the experienced beekeepers were mostly in agreement. There were always the jokes about if you ask 10 beekeepers a question you get 11 answers because the first guy changed his mind by the time you got back to him, but in reality, most of the information we got from them and from the books and the presenters at meetings and conferences was pretty consistent. We made our share of mistakes, many of them quite serious, but it helped us learn faster and find out what *not* to do. It also made us better teachers and mentors to others later on. We got advice from other beekeepers, but the club only met twice a year and often there wasn't anyone to ask at critical points, so we just learned on our own. This forced us to study and observe the bees themselves and start to think about not just what worked, or didn't work, but *why* it did or didn't work.

The reason I started keeping bees was simply because I love honey. I wanted to produce my own honey because I used a lot of it. I found the bees fascinating and a challenge to work. I began to develop a system that worked for me and after three years found myself able to propagate my own bees year by year without buying new packages at all. The only hitch was that every year those bees got meaner and meaner. Finally the fourth winter they all died. So I started fresh with new bees and they were gentle and good and over time I got back to where I had been, sort of. By this point things had changed in the beekeeping world, but it was hard to pinpoint what was different.

All the "experts" just kept up the same broken record "It's the varroa mite, stupid!" The funny thing was that I never had any serious issues with the varroa mite in my beekeeping experience. I had mean bees and bees that did things that didn't make sense, but the only hives that ever had any mites were hives that were weakened by chemical overspray or queenlessness. Of course the experts told me that I just was ignorant and that the mites were the real cause of everything that ever went wrong with my hives, I was just in denial that they were there.

At the same time this was going on, a new wave of beekeepers began to flood the beekeeping scene. These new people were of all ages, some young, some retirement age ready to start a second "life" and some in-between the two. All of a sudden those who attended beekeeping meetings had all colors of hair, not just gray, and even some colors that don't occur naturally! This was terrific for beekeeping. The only problem was that this new generation of beekeepers were reaching out to the internet first for their information, not bee books or club meetings. Almost in a knee-jerk reaction to this, bee clubs ramped up their formats to be more "interesting" and increased the amount of programming. Suddenly new beekeeping books flooded the market. This happened so quickly that all kinds of information burst on the scene that was constantly contradicting itself and established beekeeping literature and practice.

Then "CCD" whatever it was or is, happened. The commercial beekeepers were hit the hardest and went into a panic trying to make their businesses profitable again. They grasped at any bizarre solution or explanation to try to find the "silver bullet" to make it all better like it was before. This panic led to more misinformation and the rise of more "experts" who had the sure-fire answer that would solve it all. Each time one of these people wrote an article or gave a presentation they made it clear that anyone that held a different opinion or position was just ignorant.

Several previously respected people in the beekeeping world who advocated more natural methods of beekeeping were marginalized and pretty much disappeared from the beekeeping scene publically. It became politically incorrect to advocate any one method (especially if it didn't involve at least some "soft" method of varroa control). Everyone wanted healthy bees that overwintered well and produced a lot of honey, but no one would accept that it was possible to accomplish that without at least IPM (integrated pest management), which includes some chemical controls in the hives. Beekeepers who chose to not use varroa controls were told they were irresponsible because they were allowing this mite to run rampant and destroy other beekeeper's hives. It was their moral duty to place chemicals on their hives. It was compared to the foulbrood epidemic early in the 20th century.

So I did my part to educate new beekeepers, to show them by example how to successfully keep bees. I spent countless hours on field days, answering emails, talking on the phone. Each of the individuals I helped were very grateful and were able to apply these methods successfully to their beekeeping. Yet the established beekeeping community was not on board. The same old theme, "It's the varroa mite, stupid!" kept being played over and over again. I was ready to show that the mite was a symptom of weak hives, not a cause, and that a healthy hive could successfully combat varroa, but that was not something the established beekeeping community wanted to hear. My theory about that will unfold throughout this book, but basically it involves each of us taking responsibility for the health of our hives, not just throwing on a miticide strip now and then and calling it good.

This book is my answer to the establishment. I hope that by writing it all out in one volume it will become accessible to a larger number of beekeepers, so that the impossible will be possible once again and one by one we will take back the beekeeping world and bring the honeybee back to its former glory, with a honey pot on every table!

Chapter 1
The Big Picture

I have attempted to garden most of my life. I never took any classes, I just started planting seeds and watching what they did from a young age. I picked up a lot of information through the years by listening to older gardeners, reading books and mostly by observing nature. One thing I picked up over time was that even in my (semi) managed garden, nature would restore any imbalance that occurred, either through my mismanagement or natural disaster. I observed that healthy plants didn't get insect pests on them, while stressed plants did, even in the same row. This observation has been made by other gardeners as well. I also observed that when the plants recovered from their stress they again reached an equilibrium and could combat insects and disease once more. Most stressors were obvious – flooding or too many weeds. When the garden dried out or the gardener cleared the weeds, the plants once again thrived.

But wait, you say, this is a book about bees, who cares about gardens? First of all, bees cannot live without plants, so the more you understand about plants, the more you can understand about bees. Secondly, it became apparent to me that the observations I made about plants were also applicable on several levels to my bees. In my personal experience, healthy bees combat pests and disease. The presence of pests and disease in a beehive is an indication that the bees are stressed and thus weak. Correcting the stressor will often bring about the natural balance of the hive and the pests and/or disease will disappear naturally.

Could it really be that easy? I believe it is. Bees are not domesticated animals, although I know for a fact some beekeepers believe that they are. They are wild insects. They are not only insects, which are vastly different from mammals, but they are of a very small group of insects – social insects. This means they live and die as a colony, not specifically as individuals. This adds a layer of infinite complexity to the nature of bees. Because they perform much of their daily activities far away from human observation, it is difficult for us to make absolute assumptions about their behavior. Many dedicated people have done countless hours of observations which are incredibly interesting. I am in awe of people who take the time to study these fascinating creatures to that extent. Yet, all that knowledge really doesn't make it possible to keep bees better without an understanding of the big picture of how bees live within a complex ecosystem.

We must understand what the basic needs of a colony of bees are. As with all living creatures, they need food, water and adequate shelter to survive. I live at the 43rd parallel, which means we have cold winters and low sunlight from November to March. This means that the bees must store enough food and have adequate enough shelter to survive the winter. Feral colonies figure this out on their own and seem to survive. Managed colonies have an added stressor – the beekeeper.

I know when I was a new beekeeper I wanted to spend a lot of time with my bees. I opened the hive once a week and worried and stressed over my bees. They responded by stressing themselves. They superseded their queen, they swarmed, they went queenless, they got grumpy and mean and some absconded. Gradually I relaxed and let them manage themselves. I checked them more from the outside than inside, learning to recognize what was normal behavior and what looked odd and needed attention. I did my best to only get in the hives once a month, except for during critical periods. This seemed to pay off in healthier, more productive hives for me.

I also learned that the bees need food to live. In the warm months that means adequate forage. I originally had most of my hives in my yard. They did OK, but always had trouble with stress. I moved them to the edge of the woods where there are a lot of basswood trees and open fields of wildflowers and unmanaged wild plants. Now they thrive. My other hives are in the middle of a hay field and on the edge of a wild swamp. There are managed farm fields nearby, but the wild areas are closer and more abundant. On an average to poor year I get 60 pounds of honey per hive, on a good year as much as a hundred or more. That's with leaving enough honey for the bees to overwinter – all the way until the flowers bloom in the spring.

In the winter and spring bees need honey. I know beekeepers have fed sugar water for over 100 years, but dairy people have fed calves milk replacer for almost as long, too. Do they live? Yes. Do they thrive? My personal opinion on both counts is no. If a beekeeper manages the hives properly the only time a hive will ever need sugar water is a newly established hive that is set up too early in the season for natural forage to be available. Technically, that could (and probably should) be avoided as well, by just waiting until natural forage is available to start a new hive. The bees do. Natural swarming season in our region is May and June. Beekeepers start package bees in April, sometimes late March. We often still have snow on the ground at the end of March. That's sort of like planting a tomato plant in my garden on April first. Where I live that would not be a wise gardening choice.

Population density is also something to think about. I have never seen 25 feral colonies in one area. Usually there are only a few. I personally try to keep five colonies or less in any one location. That will seem impossibly extreme to some people. I am not writing a treatise on how to keep bees commercially. Obviously I have different goals. I want to produce enough honey for my family to consume. If I have extra, I sell it. I do have extra, and you can too, with even five hives or less. Sometimes small is beautiful, and when there are fewer hives in an area, it stands to reason there is more forage to go around. We had an apiary for our local bee club in a location where there were a lot of commercial plant nurseries. We had five hives and there were two more in that location that belonged to the son of the property owner. At the end of the summer, our hives were light and his were heavy. His bees had robbed out our hives! There wasn't much natural forage in the area because there was too much managed agriculture. There were too many hives for the inadequate forage, so the strong robbed the weak and he had a nice crop of honey! We learned our lesson and moved the hives to a location where there was more natural forage. The bees did much better there.

It is the beekeeper's responsibility to place hives in locations with adequate and healthy forage for the bees. Beehives are relatively small and easy to move. Much easier than say, a cow barn. So, if a location is not working, as I described above, the hives should be moved to a more appropriate location. So what exactly constitutes an appropriate location? Remember the basics that all creatures need to live – food, water and shelter. Think about these things in light of long term relationships. For instance, our experimental apiary was in front of a swamp. Even in a drought year that apiary produced adequate honey, both for itself and extra for us. Why? Because it had adequate food and water. The swamp never dried up, even in a dry season, so there was always something growing and blooming around it. It may have been different forage than the bees used in a less extreme year, but it was adequate for their needs.

As realtors say, it is all about location, location, location. Weather changes-- some years are wet, some are dry, some are cold, some are hot. Choose a location that is going to work in any type of weather. Don't put hives in low spots which could possibly flood, even if only in hundred year floods. Murphy's Law states that the hundredth year is the year you put your hive there. Don't place hives directly under trees that could drop limbs (or fall themselves) on your hives. Don't place them in a barren, open area exposed to extreme winds – especially winter winds. Place them where they get eastern or southern exposure to the sun on the front entrance, so the bees can get up and moving earlier in the morning, and in the winter can receive the benefit of any sunlight there is. In short, give them some type of protection from prevailing winds, especially winter winds, and exposure to sun, especially winter sun in cold climates.

Some things will be location specific. For instance if your area has bears, you need to protect the hives from them. You need to either fence the hives or place them on elevated platforms. I don't have to deal with this myself, but it seems like putting the hives up on a platform would limit the ability of the beekeeper to work them properly. I personally would use a fence. On this same line, don't place hives in a heavy traffic zone for large animals like deer. I have had beehives knocked sideways by startled deer. Also protect the hive from skunks and from mice in the winter. There are many methods for doing this, just choose one and do it if it is a problem in your area.

A location can be tested by having at least two hives in any one area. If both do poorly, there is something wrong with the location. If one does well and the other not so well, it may just be the bees. Give a location a whole season with at least two hives to test it out. Sometimes there are things you never thought about that become apparent over time. My best location was used in the past by an experienced beekeeper for years. He knew what worked, and I knew he kept an average of ten hives in that location throughout the time he kept bees. I found it was in fact an excellent location and successfully kept three or four hives there for several years. Unfortunately we had to give up that location when the property owner decided to activate the gravel pit and crushed concrete for a month during beekeeping season. The resulting dust was too much for the bees and they perished over the winter. So, once again, we moved the hives, it was disappointing, but not impossible by any means.

Do I need to know exactly what makes a perfect environment for my bees to choose a location? In short, no. Try a location out, evaluate it based on hive strength, honey production and successful overwintering. If it fails the test, MOVE THE HIVES. The simple thing is to not keep doing something that doesn't work. Keep trying and making one change at a time – not too many changes at once, or you won't know what is making it fail – until you find a location that works for the bees and for yourself. A location must be convenient for you to access and check the bees or you won't get out there at critical times.

Chapter 2
Does it really have to be that hard?

Beekeepers today are repeatedly told that keeping bees is much harder today than it was in the past. For the experienced beekeeper it is depressing, but for the beginner it can be enough to make one just give up. I have read a lot of older beekeeping books, written between the turn of the 20th century and the 1930's or so. Except for references to comb honey systems which are no longer used, there is very little that seems different to me in the challenges and systems used by the beekeepers. Every debate and argument put out in the past is what we hear today in modern bee meetings. The big difference is that beekeepers in the past were concerned with external poisoning threats to their hives and would react to foulbrood and other diseases and pests like wax moths with mechanical methods, such as burning equipment or cleaning it thoroughly. The idea of adding chemical contaminants directly to the hives to control pests or diseases was not considered.

One may argue that in this scientific age we know more about pests and diseases and can control them better now because they did not have the science and resources available to them at that time. However, fruit and vegetable growers were already using quite dangerous chemicals on their plants during that time period to control insects. Beekeepers were fighting adulteration and fighting for pure food laws. The last thing they wanted to do was contaminate their own pure product! In fact, the reason comb honey was produced in such quantity and was so popular with the public was because there was no way to adulterate or fake it. The public knew they were getting something absolutely pure. The beekeepers put a lot of effort into getting the bees to make the comb honey in boxes that could be scraped and packaged right up for sale. What beekeeper in their right mind would put poison in the hives, with the possibility of contaminating the honey?

So, was it easier to keep bees a hundred years ago? I think not. I do think that beekeepers expected it to be hard work and accepted that as part of the beekeeping experience. To me, it seemed that the most successful beekeepers were those who were good students of the bees and of the natural environment in which the bees live. They took the time to watch carefully and evaluate over time what worked for the bees and what environmental factors were good for the bees and what were bad. They also paid close attention to their physical location and worked with the bees and the seasons. Transportation was more difficult in those days, so a beekeeper would keep his or her bees in one type of environment – not moving from the northern part of the US to Florida and back each year. This does not mean they didn't keep thirty or more hives in each beeyard and kept several beeyards in different locations, but they were all in one general location, close enough to travel to at least once a month or so. Some beekeepers would move all their hives into cellars for the winter. That certainly couldn't have been easy. I can't imagine doing that, especially for thirty or more hives! Then they had to monitor them all winter long to make sure they didn't break dormancy and fly around. They also had to make sure they had adequate ventilation to keep from suffocating.

So why do we perceive it to be so much harder now? The main reason is that the failure cycle keeps beekeepers of all levels of experience and hive numbers in a perpetual state of discouragement. The big question is: Do we have more failure now than in the past, and if so, why? The second question is: Is this failure increasing or decreasing the more we find "solutions" for it? I do think the failure level is higher today than for beekeepers a hundred years ago. I also think the failure level is increasing the more we come up with novel "solutions" for the problems. My personal feeling is that we haven't identified the root reasons for failure, or if we have we refuse to believe it because we don't want to do what it takes to fix it. We want beekeeping to be easy. We live in the modern age of science that makes everything accessible by the flip of a switch or a push of a button. We don't want to accept that beekeeping has changed very little in a hundred years because it isn't possible to mechanize it. Maybe the answer lies somewhere between the past and the present and is simpler than we think.

There is an old saying that says, "The more things change, the more they stay the same." Each generation thinks it is smarter and better than the one before and discounts anything the former generation has to say. This limits our ability to learn from the past and make use of what has already been done successfully, or has already proven to be a failure. We waste countless hours, days and years basically "reinventing the wheel"-- repeating the same trials and errors that have already been done over and over before simply because we are too arrogant to look to the past and read what was written and acknowledge that we are no different than those who preceded us. I personally enjoy reading old beekeeping books and journals. I am privileged to have a large collection of old bee magazines dating back to 1916. Some of the books I have read seem so contemporary I have to check the copyright to be sure it was really written a hundred years ago. Some of the information is useful, some entertaining and some I am sure is not useful, but it is absolutely the same today. It is up to me to sift through the information and use my own common sense and personal experience to weed out what is useful from what is not. In a short word, I am obligated to THINK.

This process of thinking has led me to consider that there are many factors that lead to the success or failure of beehives or any other agricultural venture. A large proportion of those factors are out of my control, so it is important that I positively identify what is in my control and make sure I create the most positive, healthy environment I can for my bees. I have discovered that less is more, and that the harder it is, the more likely it is that I am doing something that is more destructive than helpful. It seems to me that the simpler I make the process, the more success I have. Ultimately I have to give the bees the best chance to be successful themselves, with as little input from me as possible. The nice thing about that is that it is less stressful for both of us, me and the bees. It allows me to focus on the positive and to also be able to focus on other agricultural activities that complement the bees and beekeeping.

Chapter 3
First Things First

I have spent a lot of time giving background and philosophy, so now let's get down to the practical part of how to make it work. I know many people reading this are experienced beekeepers, but I must take a bit of space to explain the basics of honeybee biology, because although most of us know the basics, we may never have thought much about how that affects our management of the hives.

We all know there are three types of bees in the hive, the queen (usually only one), the workers and the drones. I am not writing a detailed book on biology, so I will be brief here. The queen is the mother of all the bees in the hive, and her personality will have great effect on the overall mood of the hive. However, she does mate with as many as 21 drones according to experts, so the workers of the hive also can carry the traits of their fathers. I will talk about that angle as well. The workers are the females who do all the work of the hive and are the largest population in the hive. The drones are the sting-less males who exist for the sole purpose of mating queens. Now obviously they aren't mating the queen in their hive because she has already mated once for life. Their purpose is to mate virgin queens from other hives, most researchers believe, not necessarily a sister virgin from their own hive.

A lot of research has gone into queen breeding. Everyone wants to save the bees by breeding super queens who will conquer all pests and diseases once and for all by their excellent genetics. The problem with focusing on just queen breeding is that queens do best with open mating. Yes, they can be artificially inseminated, but that is risky and often produces less than ideal results. How can the researcher absolutely control every drone with which the queen mates? They try to do these experiments in isolated areas where they think they know they have control of the bee population, but how can one really know? Some of the most successful beekeepers allow the queens to open breed and try a different tact – increasing good drone production.

Current trends are to limit drone production for several reasons. The first is that drones are seen as a liability to the hive and are not productive. For this reason, all foundation is sized with worker cell imprints so that the bees have to make drone comb on edges or in empty spaces or build it up off the foundation to fit it in. Because this is harder for the bees, fewer drones are produced than in a hive with natural comb. The second reason for limiting drone production is that the varroa mite prefers to incubate in drone cells. So, beekeepers are encouraged to allow drones to be developed, then to destroy the larva during development to control the varroa population. Many beekeepers equate too many drone cells with an unproductive queen. They want lots of workers who will make lots of honey or do lots of pollination work.

Think about how bees reproduce on the individual level, not the hive level. One queen bee mates with as many as 21 drones. So, if you were thinking in terms of genetic statistics, which type of bee has more impact on future generations – one queen, or 21 drones? In the past, successful beekeepers encouraged drone production in their strongest, best hives so they would put a lot of good drones out into the breeding pool to breed virgin queens. I think the key to increasing genetic diversity and developing stronger, healthier bees is to flood the areas where we live with good, strong drones from survivor hives. I have started using foundationless frames so the bees can make natural comb in my hives. One of the big advantages of this method is that I have a lot more drones. As each year goes by, I have

Foundationless Brood Frame

better success with splits and nucleus hives (nucs) which I allow to make their own new queens, and I have better overwinter survival. Given the choice on how to make and arrange their own comb, the bees will produce both worker and drone brood in the combs, with the drones in the middle and the workers on the outside. It is fascinating to see how they arrange a frame when given the opportunity to do it their own way, rather than to follow a man-made pattern imprinted on foundation sheets.

Another thought on queen breeding —by its very nature, breeding for a certain trait limits genetic diversity. Bees are very susceptible to a narrowing of the gene pool because of the

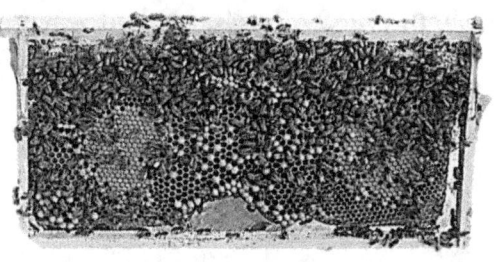

Layout of a Foundationless Brood Frame

die off in the 1980's with the varroa mite, the limits on importing bees from other countries due to the fear of pests and dis-

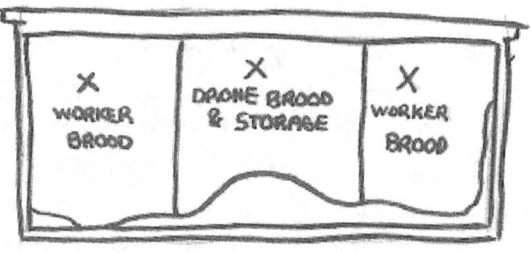

eases, and because the bees themselves have drones which only have one strand of DNA because they develop from unfertilized eggs. Since they are already so vulnerable to this shallow gene pool, it would seem unwise to narrow it further by attempting to breed queens with certain desirable traits. By letting the bees make their own queens in a location over a period of years, adapted bees will naturally develop. The bees themselves will accomplish this with no outside assistance – time, money or sweat and tears. The more we try to intervene, the more we make the problem worse.

A notion that was put forward to beekeepers in the past, but not heard much anymore, is this: All beekeeping is local. This means that what works for me in my location MAY NOT WORK FOR YOU. This idea of a "one size fits all" beekeeping manual, or even the bees themselves, cannot work because of the vast diversity of ecosystems and environments. Going back to plants, all growers know there is a zone system where a grower can see if a plant is hardy in their environment. This is a broad place to start and good growers know there are also things called "micro-climates". That means that there are places in my yard where one plant will grow because it is more sheltered, but in another place in my yard where it is more open the same plant cannot survive. This is true of bees as well. Bees kept in one area over a period of two or three seasons will begin to develop adaptive survivor traits for that particular locality. Because this can be so narrow, the healthiest bees are those raised very close to where you live. If you need to buy bees the best chance of success is to buy them from someone quite near to where you live.

In the past, it was common for new beekeepers to start by catching a swarm. Swarms have become less common in recent years due to the overall decline of the health of bees and the survivability of feral colonies. Also, one cannot be sure if the swarm came from the hives of the local commercial beekeeper who just returned from Florida either, so that makes it a little harder to recommend that it is the best way for a new beekeeper to start. The swarm could also have come from someone's existing hive which just started this year, not from an overwintered survivor colony. The best swarms are those that issue in May or June. The old saying went like this: "A swarm in May is worth a load of hay, a swarm in June is worth a silver spoon, a swarm in July ain't worth a fly." This is because the strongest colonies reproduce by swarming in the periods of honey flow and when there is plenty of time to prepare for the coming winter. It is probably fairly safe to collect swarms during those times if you aren't located near large fields or orchards that are pollinated by commercial beekeepers. Swarms later in the season are surely not adapted to a northern climate. They don't know there is a winter coming that they must be prepared for, so they act like they are living in a more tropical region and go about their normal "tropical" behavior. This is fine if you live in a warm region with no harsh winter, but if you live in the north, those bees are not adapted to your region.

I am not against commercial beekeepers, it is just that since they always move their bees to regions with no real winter, they have created an adapted bee for their purpose. That bee doesn't need to store up for winter, because winter never comes. They don't need to make excess honey because the beekeeper is always providing sugar water in times of dearth. The bees have adapted to a "just in time" inventory system like modern businesses. This works fine for the commercial beekeeper who makes his or her income from pollination because they need the bees to always be at full strength for foraging and pollination. They like them to be on the verge of swarming so they can make splits and increase whenever they like. However, this type of bee is not suited for the average backyard beekeeper who wants to produce honey and keep bees from year to year and not have to keep buying new bees to replenish his or her stock every season.

The big problem is that the most common way for a new beekeeper to begin a hive is to buy package bees. Because commercial beekeepers are the largest customers of bee farms, naturally the bees produced at these farms are those with traits that are most useful to the commercial beekeeper. Also, most of these bee farms are located in warmer regions, so the bees are more adapted to warm climates. These regions are also more likely to be Africanized. In fact, most of the large package bee farms are in regions that have Africanized bees. The bee farms do their best to keep the bees from being contaminated with Africanized genetics, but since queens must mate in the open, this is virtually impossible to really control. Researchers have noted that Africanized bees are more aggressive in mating, so the drones are more likely to mate a virgin queen than European drones. Even if she mates with 21 or more drones, if the majority of those are Africanized, her offspring will have Africanized characteristics.

What exactly does that look like in an average backyard bee? Well, there is no way to tell by looking at the bees or the queens if they are hybridized with Africanized genetics. Some of the behavioral traits include extreme aggressiveness, which can cause animal and human deaths. This is not always present, however, so a hive can have Africanized genetics and be nice sometimes and extremely mean at other times. However, they have a tendency to swarm a lot, to abscond – especially new packages just installed— or to kill European queens and raise their own queens. These hives are very difficult to re-queen, although experienced beekeepers are successful at it. In fact, it is the only way beekeepers in known Africanized regions can keep bees at all. They routinely re-queen with European queens, and check often to see if a new, unmarked queen is in the hive. They always make sure the queens they place in the hive are marked so they can tell if they have been superseded.

The good news/bad news for the northern beekeeper is that the Africanized bees can't survive harsh winters. I believe this is a contributing factor to poor overwintering in recent years, especially in colder regions. The bad news is the hives die off. The good news is that the nasty bees are gone, at least temporarily. I think northern beekeepers should take advantage of this situation and stop bringing in package bees and start raising local nucleus hives. Package bees are nothing new, but because of the state of beekeeping today, they have become unsustainable in northern regions. They are all produced in warmer climates during a time of year when the bees are not foraging or coming out of their winter cluster yet in the north. This brings bees to a harsh, barren environment when the adapted bees are not flying yet. The package bees often survive and do well, but it is a rough start and a risk of bringing at the least, weak genetics un-adapted to the northern environment, and the worst, Africanized genetics into the gene pool of a local area. This weakens the local gene pool and makes it more difficult to raise bees that have adapted strong genetics to survive in the region.

As a response to this type of thinking, beekeepers are raising nucleus hives (nucs) and putting southern queens with them so they are ready earlier in the season for northern beekeepers. In essence, this is the same as a package from the south, with the exception that the queen is laying and there is some comb and probably overall fewer bees. Even if the bees survived a northern winter, they will soon die and all the new bees will be daughters of the southern queen, so that is not a northern nuc at all. As I stated in the previous paragraph, part of the problem is that the packages are coming in too early in the season, with bees ready to forage and nothing to forage on. This is an artificial situation created on a calendar which was established by pollinators who want to have their bees ready for tree fruit bloom. The "average" date for tree fruit bloom in the north is mid-April (at least in our region), so that arbitrarily became the date that package bees arrive in the north. Since that date is an average, at least half of the time it is too early for the bees and nothing is blooming yet. Other years the bloom is on. It is a gamble. However, if one raises their own nucs and lets them make a queen during what would be the normal swarming season, the bees will adapt to the weather and produce the queen at the appropriate time and season so the resources are ready when the bees are.

Chapter 4
The Local Beekeeper

So, how do you become a local beekeeper? Do you even want to become a local beekeeper? I think you will find the answer to that question by determining what your goals are as a beekeeper. If you want to have an operation where you can overwinter bees success-fully, make increase year by year from your own hives, some to keep some to sell, and make plenty of honey for yourself and for your bees, you have answered yes. If you want to be in a place where you never need to buy bees again, you definitely have answered yes. Here is where the first roll of the eyes comes from the "experts". "That is impossible in today's beekeeping climate," they say. No one can have good enough winter survival to never need to buy packages or nucs. I think you can. I know I have. The path to get there is simple, but revolutionary. It is also old-school and not fashionable. It tends to lean heavily on common sense and less on science. Are you brave enough to walk that path? Are you brave enough to let nature take its course and take a more hands off approach? Will some of your bees die? Most likely, especially in the first season or two. Would your bees die anyway? Most likely, so what do you have to lose?

How does one start down this path? The first brave, revolutionary thing one must do is to find a local source for bees. If you can't get bees early in the season, be willing to wait until May or June. The last date a hive should be started in the north is the summer solstice, so don't start a hive after the end of June. I figure the 4th of July is still safe, but definitely not later than that. Find a local beekeeper who keeps bees without chemicals. This will bring on the second roll of the eyes from the experts. "You cannot successfully keep bees without chemical controls for varroa mites," they say. This is the weakest of the arguments from the experts because there are many, many beekeepers who successfully keep bees without chemicals. I will go into more detail as we go through management on that subject, but for now, just focus on finding chemical free bees. The closer the beekeeper raising your bees is to your physical location the better. There are two reasons for this: first of all, they will be more adapted to your region, and secondly, you will have a built in resource for beekeeping nearby in the person from whom you buy your bees.

The second brave, revolutionary thing you must do is think critically about every aspect of beekeeping and figure out if it is done because of convention – i.e. everyone does it, especially the "experts"--or because it really works. Secondly, does it work only in warm environments with very mild winters, or does it work in northern environments with cold winters? Thirdly, does it work without unnatural inputs from the beekeeper? Now we really get into controversial territory. What exactly is classified as "unnatural inputs"? For simplification purposes let's just define that as chemical treatments for parasites or pathogens for now. I believe it is best to eventually get to where you are also not artificially feeding and even (gasp) not using foundation. However, those are things you must gradually introduce to your beekeeping because you must start somewhere.

For instance – I have been asked many times about screened bottom boards. I started with solid bottom boards, moved to screened bottom boards for several years and now have moved back to solid bottom boards. Why? Because I found no real reason to use the screened bottom boards in actual practice and the solid bottom boards were easier to use and to make ourselves. Some antique beekeeping boxes had attached bottom boards. I can see why. It goes along with a lot of other things like: Switching brood boxes, moving honey around in the hive, re-queening on a schedule just because, cleaning off the bottom board during the winter or early spring and opening the hive in the winter to see how the bees are doing. Over time I found all of these things unnecessary. If the hive was healthy, it took care of all these things itself without my help, even cleaning off its own bottom board in the spring. The more I intervened to "help" the bees, the more I messed them up and eventually caused them to become weak.

So, the most important part of being a local beekeeper is to find local bees, then to think for yourself. This involves watching and observing how the bees act and react to different situations. It also involves a lot of patience. You must be willing to let the bees try to correct a problem before you step in to intervene. This may result in failure. You then chalk it up to experience and learn from it so you can do it differently next time. To make mistakes is definitely part of learning. To keep making the same mistakes is not learning at all. Use your failures to become a better beekeeper and a better steward of the environment. The patience part is key. Beekeeping, especially sustainable, local beekeeping takes several years to establish. Think of it like growing a fruit tree. You plant a tree and don't expect to harvest fruit for three to five years. Many times it is ten years before the tree is producing at full strength. The good news is that you can get there faster in beekeeping, but to really establish strong, local hives that can keep reproducing themselves without bringing in purchased bees from another region takes around three to five years of diligent observation and careful attention to the details of beekeeping.

Many people scornfully talk of people who take a more hands-off approach to beekeeping as "bee-havers" not bee-keepers. I guess it depends on a lot of factors, but many beekeepers are approaching beekeeping as an industry. Bees go in, honey comes out, money goes into the pocket. Beekeeping as an industry and a science leaves out a critical factor. Bees are wild creatures in a natural environment. They cannot be manipulated and controlled, even as much as agricultural animals. They are living creatures and if the circumstances become too unbearable they will simply leave, or just die. So are you a beekeeper if you choose to let the bees take care of what they do best and you do your best to keep their environment healthy for them? I think so. I think if a person wants to set up a beehive in the garden and never open it, they are probably not a true beekeeper.

But a true beekeeper cares about not only the success of the hive in terms of honey and hive products and what it can put in his or her pocket, but also the health of the bees and the ability of the bees to continue to reproduce season after season, so there will be bees in the area for our children and our grandchildren, not just until the end of this honey season.

Chapter 5
Getting Started

How do you find local bees? The best way is to find a local bee club. Most states have a state beekeeping association and have the local clubs listed on their website. Search for that for your state and then try to find a bee club as close as possible to where you live. The good news is that bee clubs are popping up all over the place now because beekeeping is becoming quite trendy. However, if this doesn't work for you, another option is to go to your local farmer's market and look for a honey vendor. Ask lots of questions. Every beekeeper does things differently. I have bought nucleus hives (nucs) from beekeepers who don't share my philosophies. That is fine. If the queen is healthy and she was produced in your local area, not brought in from somewhere else and put into a nuc, that is fine. It doesn't matter so much how the beekeeper operates that raised your nuc. The important thing is that the nuc is truly local – the bees and the queen. Ideally you want it to come from close by, within say, 20 miles, but that may not be realistic. If you can't find a nuc close by, try to find one raised in a similar region. For instance, my plant growth region is region number five, so a plant adapted to region five will grow in my yard. If the nuc is coming from some place that has a similar environment, that is good. You have to start somewhere and a nuc raised in a similar region will be better than a package from the south when you live in the north. Start your search early in the year. Often people will promise all their potential nucs long before the snow leaves the ground.

Make your decisions about location and equipment long before you get your bees. Keep in mind the importance of forage requirements. I usually recommend to new beekeepers to start with just two hives. If the bees were in better shape I would recommend you start with just one, but because of the overall weakness of the bees, you need two so you can have some insurance. The nice thing about bees is that they can make a new queen from eggs or young larva, so if one hive goes queenless, you can re-start it by giving it a frame of young brood from the other hive. This is why you need two hives. Bee-keeping takes a lot of learning up front, especially if you want to try some of my methods which go against conventional wisdom. It is easier to do this with just two hives than trying to keep up with ten when you don't have your methods figured out yet.

Since I have covered location already, I will talk about equipment. The bees will basically adapt to whatever you put them in. Bees have been found in the most amazing places when a swarm finds a new home. What you want to think about in equipment is what works best for you. You want it to be convenient, so you can get out and do what needs to be done in the hives in a timely fashion. You want it to be easy for you to manage physically. Think about whether you will have someone helping you keep bees, or if you are doing all the management alone. This will greatly affect what equipment you choose. What is your ultimate goal in beekeeping? Do you just want a couple of hives for a hobby, or do you eventually want a whole lot for honey production as a sideline business?

First of all, I recommend that you use standard Langstroth frames and boxes that will fit them. Although this sounds obvious, there are a lot of other designs out there. I have successfully used Lang-stroth frames without foundation to get natural comb, and have put them in a horizontal box that acts like a top bar hive. The frames are interchangeable with standard Langstroth equipment, so I can make splits and put them in regular vertical hives and I can transfer frames back and forth. I feel that the flexibility of the standardized frame size is very important. In reading older bee literature one of the biggest complaints was the in-compatibility of equipment. Once one started with one manufacturer, he had to stick

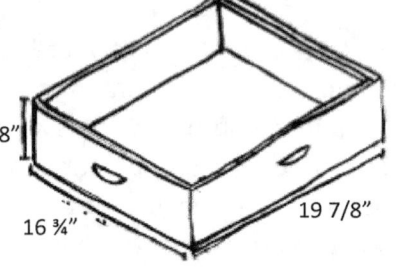

5 3/8"

16 ¾"

19 7/8"

Shallow Honey Super

with that or buy all new equipment. All American bee-keeping suppliers use the same Langstroth standards now, so you can interchange equipment regardless of where you buy it from. You can also make your own. It is easier to make boxes than frames, so it is very handy that the frames will fit no matter who makes them. I think this is just common sense and will save you a lot of headaches in the future. You can experiment with configurations, just use standard measurements.

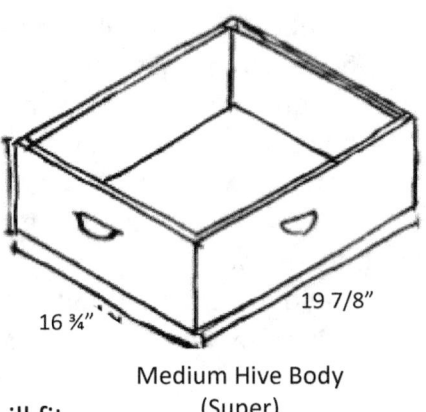

6 5/8"

19 7/8"

16 ¾"

Medium Hive Body
(Super)

If you are planning on having a large apiary and eventually making a business, you will benefit from having most of your boxes the same size. Many beekeepers are switching to all medium-depth boxes. This way the brood frames can be moved down to the brood boxes and the honey frames kept up in the honey boxes and all boxes and frames are the same size. They are also significantly lighter and eas-ier to manipulate than deep boxes. Many hobby beekeepers are doing the same for the sake of convenience. I had switched to all mediums until I started experi-menting with long hives, which use deep frames. Now I keep some deeps around for splits off the long hives, but otherwise I use mostly medium boxes.

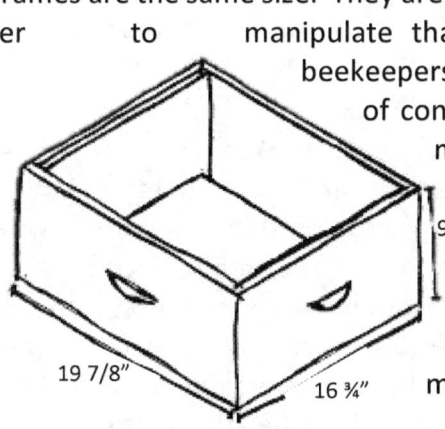

9 5/8"

19 7/8"

16 ¾"

Langstroth Deep Hive Body

There are eight frame hives avail-able. For a less physically strong beekeeper, especially if he or she is keeping bees alone, eight frame mediums are even lighter and easier to handle. Just make sure you order the right sized inner covers, top covers and bottom boards to fit the eight frame boxes. The horizontal hives I have been experimenting with require no lifting at all, so for someone who prefers not to lift or cannot lift heavy boxes, the most one ever needs to lift is one deep frame, which shouldn't weigh more than ten pounds. I place these hives at waist level, so there is no real bending, either. I also use a hinged lid so all the beekeeper has to do is open the lid up and it stays open while he or she inspects the hive.

The next decision one must make is about foundation. All beekeepers used to use wax foundation. It is certainly the bees' favorite. Bees actually draw the comb out from the wax on the foundation sheet, so they do not need to make new wax to make the comb. Beekeepers like this because then all the nectar goes into honey production instead of wax production. The problem in recent years is that most of the wax used to make

Partially drawn out deep foundationless frame

foundation comes from large commercial beekeepers. These beekeepers use a variety of chemicals to control varroa mites and other pests and diseases in the hives. These chemicals build up in the wax. When the wax is heated, they can change form and become even more toxic. All this wax is mixed together and the chemicals can synergize to produce even more powerful toxins. This is then introduced into a beehive with a weak new package of bees. The resulting slow release of the chemicals creates a situation when the bees seem fine at first, but slowly decline over the beekeeping season. Because there is really no way to get clean wax foundation unless you make your own, most beekeepers have to switch to option B, which is plastic foundation. Plastic foundation is usually imprinted with the cell shape of a worker cell, like wax foundation. It is then coated with a thin coat of beeswax. Usually this is not enough wax to cause serious contamination in the hive. The problem is that the bees don't always like plastic foundation. It isn't that they are "plastiphobes", it is just that they want to draw out the wax into comb and there is hardly any wax there to draw out. This means they must make wax and put the comb on the foundation. If there is a good honey flow on, they will do this, but if it is a dearth or a weak flow, they will just pack the honey into every little bit of already drawn comb they have rather than draw out the plastic foundation. I have even had bees abscond, or leave the hive, rather than draw out plastic foundation. My solution to the problem has been option C – foundationless frames. One bee manufacturer – Walter T. Kelly--sells frames with a triangular comb guide in the top bar. The bees do not need anything else, they will build comb in the frames using only that wooden guide. However, the hive must be kept level. Since this is hard to do, I have found that it is helpful to place drawn comb between the empty foundationless frames to get them to draw the comb straight, not cross comb between frames. Once it is complete and attached to the frame, I can place the comb anywhere in the hive.

Foundationless frames and natural comb have a few fans and lots of critics. I was told, "You cannot extract natural comb." I was also told that I would get too many drones, that the comb wouldn't be straight in the frames and that I would get hardly any honey because the bees would have to be constantly making comb and putting all their resources into that rather than into honey. The fans on the other hand like natural comb because they think it is letting the bees do what they want, not what the beekeeper wants, and reduces contaminants in the hive. This is what I found in reality – it is somewhere in the middle. I have successfully extracted both deep and medium foundationless frames. The deeps are trickier and more prone to "blow out". The mediums, especially in a hand-cranked tangential extractor, rarely have any more difficulty than wax foundation frames. I also had to rethink what was so terrible about crushing and straining honey comb or making cut comb. I found that the crush and strain method produced an exquisite honey with no tiny bubbles like the honey from an extractor. I also got a lot more wax to use for rendering and ultimately to use for making cosmetics. I like having more wax but not everyone does. I also like the idea of having as much wax as I could possibly want for myself and even some extra to sell if I want. The cut comb aspect was also something I hadn't considered. In normal cut comb, you would use a thin sheet of foundation wax in the frame. This of course, stays in your comb for the consumer to eat. I have no idea how contaminated that wax is. That is a little frightening to me. With my natural comb, every bit of the cut comb honey is produced by my bees under my care, so I know for sure what has or hasn't been introduced into the hive by humans. The natural comb gives me the choice with each frame to extract, to use for cut comb, or to crush and strain. If I have a beautiful frame of honey I want to use for cut comb, I can. With plastic or regular wax foundation that would not be an option.

Interspersing drawn comb and empty foundationless frames—every other

I do have some problems with cross-combing. This is when the bees attach the top of the comb to one frame and the bottom to the next. This is a problem because the frames cannot be removed without damaging the comb. For an experienced beekeeper who already has drawn comb, this is easily solved by interspersing drawn comb between the empty foundationless frames. A new beekeeper can use frames with plastic foundation between the foundationless frames just to guide the combs to be straight, then replace the plastic with drawn comb when there are enough. Keeping the hive as level as possible helps, but with vertical hives it gets harder and harder to keep it level the taller the hive gets. However, a super of badly cross-combed frames can be crushed and strained, then the frames re-used again as I just described. Once the comb is made straight in the frame, it can be treated just as if it had foundation under it. It can be extracted and re-used in the hive.

I do have more drones, this is definitely true. But, just like the idea of thinking about other ways to use honey than just extracting, I had to ask myself, "Is this so bad?" As I have already stated, I think not. I think it is good to have a strong drone population and if a hive is mostly or completely full of natural comb, they will only make as many or as few drones as they think they need. The larger cells are then emptied out as the season progresses and are used for honey storage because they are bigger. So, what may seem negative is really just different than what we have been doing for so many years and not really a big deal. As far as overall honey production, I haven't noticed a marked difference. I have been gradually replacing all foundation for the past four years and have started new hives with just natural comb. I still have quite a lot of drawn comb with foundation under it, but except for the cell size, the bees see little difference between it and natural comb, especially once it is already drawn out. Besides, I really think the bees have to do almost as much work to draw out new plastic foundation because all they have to start is the foundation and a very thin sheet of wax.

I do not think the bees sit around and philosophize about what kind of frames/foundation or housing they are in. I think they adapt to what they have and just go about doing what they are intended to do – make their home, make comb for the queen to lay eggs and collect nectar and pollen and place it in cells. However, they need to evaporate the nectar to make it into honey, they need to keep the brood nest optimum temperature and they need to have room to make the comb for the queen to lay and to store nectar and pollen. As beekeepers, we need to make sure we aren't making their jobs harder than they need to be. Obviously wax foundation is the easiest for the bees. But if it is contaminated with chemicals and pathogens, it weakens the bees, making their job harder. So, for frames, I try to make it as easy and healthy for the bees as I can by letting them make natural comb in frames. I don't think they care so much, but they do seem to make the comb faster if they can do it themselves rather than having to follow the imprint on plastic frames. All factors that apply to getting bees to draw out any comb apply to foundationless frames. Bees will only make wax during honey flows. They simply do not have the resources or the need to do so at other times. So, only add empty frames to be drawn when there are lots of resources coming in and the bees need to store those resources or make more room for the queen to lay eggs.

3-inch spacer above notched inner cover on a new split.

Arrows in both pictures are pointing to ventilation holes in notched inner covers

The other main key component is ventilation. The hive must have good air flow. In the summer, the bees are bringing in nectar then evaporating it to 18% water. That is a lot of moisture they must get out of the hive. Add to that the naturally occurring humidity most regions experience in the summer, and you see that your hive must have adequate air flow. This can be accomplished by having a wide open entrance and

also ventilation at the top of the hive for warm moist air to escape. I do this by having a fully open bottom entrance on my vertical hives and using notched inner covers on the top. I use a spacer about 3" high on top of the notched inner cover to keep the telescoping top cover from covering the notch in the inner cover. There are a lot of other ways to accomplish the same goal, how you do it is not important, just that you do it. I have also observed that year-round foam insulation can make the hive too air-tight and cause mold build up in the summer. Wood breathes. I do like to use insulation in the winter, but I like it to be removable so the hive can breathe as much as possible in the summer when it needs to shed so much moisture. A healthy hive should never have mold in the summer and ideally little to none in the winter if it is properly ventilated. This often takes a bit of trial and error to figure out for your region and your particular hive design. After three years of experimentation with the horizontal Langstroth design, I have an entrance that is eight inches wide in the front and use three notched inner covers on top, rather than the one notched inner cover on the vertical hives. This seems to provide adequate ventilation both summer and winter for that hive design for me. I do have a double-walled horizontal Langstroth with natural wood shavings between the wood walls for insulation. That hive breathes adequately without collecting excess moisture. I believe the key to year-round insulation is using materials that can breathe, ideally natural materials.

So, the bottom line is to choose a good location and to get equipment that suits your physical abilities now and in the future, and also fits what your beekeeping goals are. Boxes and hive bodies can be built with a rudimentary understanding of woodworking. I never thought I could do it, but found it wasn't as hard as I thought it was. Keep things as simple as possible. Like I said, I came full circle on solid vs. screened bottom boards because in my personal experience it made very little difference. Solid bottom boards are much easier to build, either from scratch, or in pieces from a dealer. They last a lot longer because there is more wood to rot away. If you make your own, you can use a more rot resistant wood (not treated wood, please!). I like the short hive stands with the angled alighting board for the bees to walk up into the hive entrance. I don't like tall hive stands. Again, this is personal preference. I am just over five feet tall, and as soon as my hives get over six supers high, I am struggling to see inside already. I don't need them up an extra eight or ten inches! Think about these things. Why do hives need to be elevated off the ground any-way? The short stands I use just keep the bottom board from touch-

ing the ground so they take longer to rot away. It also gives the bees that nice little "runway" to carry their heavily laden bodies up to the en-trance when a good flow is on. Don't make things harder on yourself than you have to. As I have stated, the bees care very little about some of these things, they are

Preparing a site for a Long Langstroth Hive using sand, patio blocks and cinder blocks.

mostly for you. Make it as easy on yourself as possible so you can keep a better eye on how your bees are doing. I have also found it is easier to keep the entrance of the hive clear from vegetation if the hive is set on a concrete patio block foundation. This can be one 18" square block, or a combination of smaller blocks. It doesn't need to be much larger than the hive's stand, but a little around the outside makes it easier to manage in muddy weather and to keep the grass/weeds down around the hive. I learned recently that if I take a bag of playground sand out to the site, spread it out to make a level surface, then place the blocks, I can make an easy, nice level surface on which to place my hives. This is easier than leveling the ground. Level hives are easier to manage the foundationless frames.

On that same line, it is a good idea to paint or treat the outside of your equipment to protect it from the weather. I have hive boxes I bought used which are forty years old and are still useable. Make sure you do not paint or treat the inside surfaces of boxes and covers, and never treat frames or any other piece of equipment which will be inside the hive. I use latex paint. I started using interior paint just because I had it around. I found it worked perfectly fine on the bee-hives, even though it was labeled for interior use. I make it a habit to go to any place that sells paint and look on their "oops" paint rack and buy interior latex. I learned one day by looking at the label of exterior latex paint that you DO NOT want to use exterior latex on hives because insecticide is included in the paint. That is the only difference between interior and exterior latex. It pays to read the label, I discovered. Never buy or take used frames from another bee-keeper. Frames can carry disease or pathogens and you do not want to risk introducing that to your hive. Frames are relatively inexpen-sive, especially if you are not using foundation. If you choose to buy used boxes, you can lightly scorch the inside with a torch to kill dis-ease pathogens. If you want to be really safe, just buy or make new equipment. If you take proper care of it, it will last for many years. However, if your equipment becomes contaminated, please do not hesitate to destroy it – burning is best – because the small loss of equipment will be much better than spreading a dangerous disease like foulbrood. My philosophy is "when in doubt, throw it out". I try not to be paranoid, but I don't like the idea of bleaching frames or treating them with lye and putting them back in the beehive. The cure sounds worse than the cause to me. If you are getting a nucleus hive (nuc) from another beekeeper, try to make sure the nuc is on new comb, not used comb. This is hard and tricky. It is one of the disadvantages of relying on nucs rather than packages, but it is a risk I think we will have to take to get the bee population back to a healthy state.

Chapter 6
What do you REALLY need?

All the beekeeping suppliers have essential "kits" ready for you to buy. If you have ever started in any hobby you will discover quickly that while these kits have some things that you really need, there are some things you definitely could do without and some you may never use at all. I spent a lot of time explaining what you need to consider when planning your hives and what you want to do to get the bees. Now let's discuss what is really necessary for keeping the bees throughout the season. As with all hobbies that involve a tool set, it is a good idea to think ahead about how you will keep these tools organized and available when you need them. I will share some ideas about that. Many beekeepers joke that they have a dozen hive tools because they lose them all the time. One manufacturer even makes a magnetic belt to keep your hive tool handy (don't get it too close to your smart phone!). I still have my first hive tool. You can be organized, it is possible. I know it is harder for some people than for others. I have a tool tote I picked up inexpensively at the local farm store in which I keep my small tools and essentials. A friend and fellow beekeeper gave me a metal bucket that is large enough to transport and store my smoker in so I don't have to worry about it tipping over and starting a fire. I keep a bucket of smoker fuel and a box that stores my lighter and "kindling". Now let's get to the nitty gritty.

Smoker and Storage Bucket

I do think beekeepers should have a full bee suit. Whether or not you use it is up to you. I have heard countless stories of people who worked bees for years and suddenly one day had a serious reaction to a bee sting. I personally feel much more calm and at ease in my bee suit. I also wear gloves. This is up to you, but have a pair on hand, a nice pair of goatskin gloves that allow ease of movement. I have watched beekeepers who use medical gloves during their hive inspections, and they get stung repeatedly. It does not appear to be enjoyable beekeeping for them. Beekeeping is supposed to be fun, not torture. If you get hot, buy a ventilated suit. My suit is very stained with propolis. Every time I wash it and it comes out looking as dirty as it went in, I remind myself that my clothing could be stained and ruined instead if I didn't wear my bee suit. So, if you aren't going to wear a suit, be prepared to dedicate a set of clothes that will never be clean again just to beekeeping. I personally think it is easier to just wear a bee suit. If you don't use it yourself, it is nice to have on hand if someone is curious to see what beekeeping is like. If you do use your suit, consider having an extra on hand for curious on-lookers. You can buy inexpensive Tyvek suits for that purpose.

Another common question is whether or not to smoke the bees. I think that all beekeepers should have a smoker and know how to use it. It is easier to keep a smoker lit if you buy a medium sized smoker rather than the smallest size available. I personally use sumac for my main fuel and use wood shavings and newspaper for "kindling" to start it. I have a beekeeper friend who is allergic to sumac. When he is around and I am using the smoker, I use pine needles. They have more creosote, so they aren't my first choice, but they work. I have matches in my smoker box, but usually use a long lighter designed for lighting a barbeque grill. I keep extra lighters in my box. I store the smoker in the metal bucket, which I can turn upside down and use as a stand to safely light the smoker if I am in a dry field. Some people snuff the smoker when they are done with a cork. It doesn't work for me, so I usually leave mine outside until it cools down, or I put it in the bucket in a place where it is not close to anything combustible. I store the fuel in a plastic bucket with a lid. This helps keep excess humidity from making it so wet it won't burn. I store the wood chips in another plastic container and keep the newspaper and lighters and some of the other fuel in a small cardboard box that I can take with me to the hives. Now, about the question of whether you should actually smoke the bees or not – my preference is to always have the smoker lit and ready to use, but to only use it if necessary. Usually, as in everything, Murphy's Law is again at work and if the smoker is going great, I never need it, but if I can't keep it lit, the bees are grumpy. I don't smoke the hive at first. I only bring it over if the bees start flying at me aggressively. In the past several seasons I rarely have actually needed my smoker.

The other basic tool you absolutely must have is a hive tool. For years

I just had the traditional pry-bar type tool. An experienced beekeeper friend kept making fun of me because the way I was loosening the frames in the hives was placing too much pressure on the side of the hive body and causing damage. Not being too proud to change an old

Regular Hive Tool and "J" tool

habit, I bought a "J" tool and re-learned how to remove frames from the hive. It took a few weeks to establish a new and better habit, but my boxes are much happier now. It is a little harder on the frames, and any poor nailing jobs make themselves very evident very quickly, but that is all part of the learning process. Frames must have a cross nail from the side bar into the top bar under the top bar to make them stable, otherwise the prying will take the top bar right off the frames. Propolis is harder than wood, especially in cooler weather!

Other tools that I have in my basic tool kit are:

- A bee brush for brushing bees off full honey frames,
- A hand staple gun for stapling hardware cloth

over holes/entrances and for stapling winter insulation
- A pair of scissors for cutting insulation
- A pocket knife for anything too small for a hive tool
- A wire cutter/snipper for cutting hardware cloth
- Small pruners or hedge trimmers for cutting brush around the hives.

Other things other beekeepers have found useful are:

- A head lamp for looking in cells to find eggs/larva
- A magnifying glass if you are not blessed with terrific eyesight or a young person to identify eggs/larva for you

As you continue through the years as a beekeeper you will discover what you really use and what is not really necessary. Most beekeepers find they really only use a small number of tools, like the smoker and hive tool and bee brush on a regular basis. Some people only use things like a screwdriver instead of a hive tool. Whatever works for you and keeps your equipment from getting ruined, is great. There are no hard and fast rules. Do try to keep them organized and in a form that is easy to tote. Some beekeepers keep everything in their primary vehicle at all times, especially during swarm season just in case they get a swarm call. That is great too. Some people would put a cell phone on this list just in case you have a serious sting reaction. I say do what makes you feel comfortable. Thousands of beekeepers have kept bees for hundreds or thousands of years without cell phones. It is pleasanter and probably wise to take a second person along when you get into the hives, but for many people that is not an option.

The last thing you should have is some way to record in a very basic way what you do in your hives. This doesn't have to be elaborate or excessively detailed, but even with only two hives you will forget what you did last month or what the hive looked like. I keep a basic journal in a notebook and record after each hive inspection what I found in each hive and also record honey harvests. For many people it is not a habit to keep a journal like this. I admit my garden journal is sadly lacking, but my bee journal is up to date. It is more necessary with the bees. You will learn what works and what doesn't a lot faster if you record what you do and what you see. Eventually you will discover what works and what doesn't and can tailor your bee-keeping accordingly. Do this however you like, on paper or electron-ically-- whatever is easiest for you-- but do it. You will save yourself a lot of wasted time and money by making a good record of what you have done in the hives. If you are a new beekeeper and see some-thing you don't know about in the hive, take a picture and share it with a more experienced beekeeper. That way he/she can see what you are talking about and will have a lot better idea of what you saw and can hopefully help you. If you are more comfortable recording with pictures, do it that way. Just make sure you label the pictures with enough information to be helpful.

Chapter 7
Early Season Management

I will start with the management of an overwintered hive. I believe part of being a good beekeeper is to learn how to manage honey stores so you will leave enough honey on the hive for the bees to eat right up until they can find natural forage. This takes some experimenting. If you find you need to feed sugar water until you get it figured out, you are not a failure as a beekeeper. The ultimate goal is to learn how to manage the honey well. Everyone has to feed sugar water on occasion. This may be due to extreme unforeseen weather or a miscalculation last season. Still try to work toward the goal of not feeding sugar water if possible. I learned in my second year of beekeeping not to open the hives too soon. In our region, spring comes in fits and spurts and we can have very nice warm days two months before our last frost date. When spring finally comes for good, it lasts about a week, then it is blazing summer. The only thing we can count on is that we can't count on the weather. So, instead of going by dates on the calendar, I learned that we have to go by flower blooms. Usually those are much more reliable. So, I never open a hive until the daffodils bloom. I make sure the daffodils on the north, shady side of the house are blooming, not the sheltered ones on the south side! This has paid off. Usually by this time, the bees are busy raising new brood, have cleaned off the bottom board and have cleaned up any nasty stuff from winter. I remove any winter wrap, take off any empty boxes – making sure they are really empty, not full of eggs --and just make sure they are alive and well. I do not look for the queen. I only need to find her evidence. If there are young larva or eggs, she is there and is fine. I have learned over the years to disturb this hive as little as possible. I look to see if there are adult drones yet. This is my indication as to whether this hive could be ready to split. I assess its strength. Did it just barely survive the winter and needs to build up, or is it booming and ready to be split? If it is, I wait until the dandelions are in full bloom, then I know they are in a nectar flow, and then I do any splitting I feel needs done.

When the dandelions are in full bloom and there are adult drones in the hive, this is the optimum time to do splits for nucleus hives to sell or for increase and/or to prevent swarming. Here is my method for doing splits—small splits-- which both provide increase and also relieve the swarming pressure on the "mother" hive. First I prepare a new location in which to move the "mother" hive. Usually this is nearby, sometimes just next door. I was taught that a split had to be less than three feet or more than three miles, but I have not found this to be the case. I set up a new hive stand and bottom board in the new location. I get a new box to house the new split. I look for a frame of brood in the "mother" hive that has eggs in it. I carefully examine the frame to be sure the queen is not on it. I have a second person also examine it to be sure she is not there. Then, I take my hive tool and break the bottom cell wall of three cells with eggs, to make room for them to produce a queen from those cells. I then place that frame in my split box. I may do this with a second frame for insurance, or just put two more frames in the box with capped brood, always making sure the queen is not on any of the frames I remove from the hive. After this, I fill in the split box with some honey frames and drawn comb or empty frames, depending on what I have and what the intended purpose of the split will be. Now, I move the "mother" hive to the new location and set the split on the hive stand the "mother" hive was on. This allows the little split to receive all the foragers from the original hive while it waits for a new queen to develop and begin laying eggs. I wait a full month before opening this new split. At that time, if it was successful at raising a new queen, all will be well; she will be present and will probably have begun laying eggs. If I want to sell it as a nucleus hive (nuc), I will do so at this point. Otherwise, I will add another box if it needs it and just keep managing it as a new hive. If I am going to sell it as a nuc, I will put less drawn comb, and more empty frames to decrease chance of contamination. I will often have the buyer bring his/her own equipment and just transfer the frames with the bees into that to also reduce chances of contamination.

To start a new hive I will either do a split as described above, or will install a nuc bought from someone else, or a package. Package bees have decreased in quality over the past decade and because the majority of them are produced in Africanized regions and are also produced mostly for commercial beekeepers who have different goals than the backyard beekeeper, I have decided to stop getting any package bees. I am intentionally not covering how to install a package here. I think they also come too early in the season for most northern beekeepers. If you must start with a package because you cannot find a source for a nuc locally, there are many resources to help you, including local bee clubs and of course, on-line videos. Everyone does it different, but it usually works regardless. However, success has been much more variable in the past few years. When I first started beekeeping I was told that I needed to start with three packages because one would do great, one so-so and one would probably fail. This did seem to be the case. A fellow beekeeper pointed out to me that even that was unacceptable, even though we were paying half of what it costs to buy packages now. Recently if I ordered packages, it was just for replacement insurance and I only got two because the prices were getting so high. The last year I bought packages I went with a friend to pick them up, she got one, I got two. Hers went queenless, one of mine absconded and one of the three built up nicely and survived. That was only one third success, certainly not acceptable for the price. I know there were many factors involved and I never contacted the seller because I don't blame him, he was just a middleman anyway. It just illustrated to me that the era of package bees for the hobby beekeeper is basically over.

To install a nuc from another beekeeper, you simply set up the hive equipment and transfer the bees from the nuc box into the hive. Most nuc boxes will have only four or five frames, so you need to fill in the hive body with enough frames to fill the box. Make sure you do not leave empty space, or the bees will fill it with comb. If this is your first hive and there is a bloom going, you do not need to feed. If, however,

Installing sugar water can

Sugar water can with burr comb around it—we left it on the hive too long.

for some reason there is nothing blooming at the moment, you may need to feed sugar water. Because I do it very infrequently, I have not invested in feeding equipment. I simply take a plastic container, punch four or five very tiny holes in the lid, fill it with sugar water at a 1:1 ratio and invert it in the corner over the top bars of the frames. I then place an empty hive body around it and put the inner and top covers on. If you have honey frames from a previous year, or another hive, put a couple of those in instead. When the bees have covered 80% of the frames in a vertical hive, add another box of either drawn comb or empty frames, whichever you have. If there is a nectar bloom going on, it is not necessary, or even wise, to artificially feed. Remove any sugar water as soon as there is adequate forage blooming near the hives. If you leave it on too long, you will attract ants. I have also seen bees develop into "welfare" bees, choosing to just take the sugar water rather than go out and forage. I have never had this happen in my own hives; my bees will not take sugar water if there is natural forage available. However, I have heard of it happening in other people's hives. If your goal is to keep bees that can sustain themselves season after season, they need to be able to feed themselves.

Continue to add boxes to new or overwintered hives when the top box is 80% filled. This is important to prevent swarming and also to give them room to store honey as it comes in and to allow the queen to expand the brood nest. A very strong hive can be split twice as described above, as long as you don't take more than two or three frames each time. You could probably take as many as ten frames from a really strong hive and not compromise honey production. The later a new split is started the less chance it will produce excess honey. A new split should not be started later than the first day of summer; certainly July 4th should be the very last date a new hive should be started in the north. This goes for swarm collection, as well. After that point, a hive cannot build up enough to make stores for overwintering. Use this date as well for comb production. If you want new comb drawn out, stop putting empty frames in the hives after the first day of summer. From that point on, the bees need to use all the nectar they gather for honey production and forcing comb production is counterproductive. This guideline is for hives you intend to make enough food for themselves without supplemental feeding for the winter. A hive can survive if it is started later and fed sugar water. If it is your first season and you absolutely can't get bees until later than the beginning of summer, don't let that stop you from getting the bees. If you have to artificially feed at first, just do it and try to manage the bees to avoid it in the future. You have to start somewhere and sometimes reality is not what we would like our ideal to be. Just work toward it in the future.

Chapter 8
Mid-season management

The early honey flows will go strictly to comb building and hive build-up. In my region this will be primarily dandelions. Very little dande-lion honey actually ends up in the honey supers, it is all used for hive build up. Near the end of June or the beginning of July, when it is time to stop build-up, the hive switches to storing honey. This usually coincides with clover bloom, other major wildflowers and tree blooms like black locust and basswood. If you have been adding boxes as the bees build, you won't be caught short at honey season. My rule is to always have enough equipment to double your hives at any time in the spring – for splits and swarms and to have enough honey supers to be able to have three boxes above your brood nest. This is how I define the brood nest in a vertical hive – if you are using all medium boxes, it would be the bottom three. If you are using deeps for brood boxes, it would be two deeps. Above that, this is my honey management system: I leave the first box over the brood boxes, which for me in my all medium hives is the fourth box from the bottom, untouched. What that means is I leave that box as my insurance for winter stores. I let the bees fill that box with honey and don't collect it. Any box above the fourth box is fair game for me to collect. Most hives end up with six or sometimes seven boxes on them. The fifth and sixth (and seventh) are for me, that fourth box is left for the bees. I begin checking for capped frames and when there are enough to make it worth my while, I pull fully capped frames from the fifth box and above. We take fully capped frames and then replace them with empty frames. If I ever collect frames that are not fully capped, they must be at least 80% capped. If they are not, we leave them in the hive. This is to insure

The fourth medium up is the bees' honey.

← →

Above that is mine to keep.

that the honey is evaporated enough to prevent fermentation. Honey must be 18% or less water content or it will ferment. Although I do own a refractometer, and it is great fun to use, it really is unnecessary if you just follow the rule to not collect frames that are not fully, or mostly, capped. We look through the top box or two of a hive, remove any fully capped frames, place them outside the hive against a tree, replace them with empty frames and close up the hive. When we have done this in all the hives in the apiary, we begin brushing the bees off the frames of honey. We have prepared empty boxes with a towel over them in our truck. We place the brushed frames of honey in the empty boxes and cover them with the towels until we have finished all the collected frames. We then transport them back to the garage and either extract immediately, or set them aside until we can get to extracting.

While we are collecting honey, we are observing the health of the hives. Before opening the hives, I always observe the hive. Is there a good amount of traffic going in and out? Is there anything that looks unusual to me? Before going out, I try to look at my journal to determine what this hive was like the last time I checked it. Is there anything I need to check on? Was it queenless last time? If so, we check for signs of a new queen – we would have followed the procedure for making a queen like I do with a split – if she isn't there, we try again. I discovered several years into beekeeping that it was not uncommon for a hive to go queenless during the honey season. I usually did not catch this because the hive can continue to store honey and act almost normal until fall, when the numbers noticeably dwindle and it is too late to save the hive. Sometimes I didn't catch it at all and thought it was a winter loss. One clue was dead drones on the bottom board in the spring. The hive should have kicked them out before winter, but in a queenless hive, they let them live in the vain hope they can produce a new queen. So, I learned that it is important to check for signs of a queen during the honey flow, so if something happened to her, you can try to get them to raise a queen before it is too late.

Always keep that first day of summer date in your mind. Now if a strong hive loses a queen in July (like maybe the beekeeper accidently killed her during an inspection – it happens), they can re-queen and still make it through the winter. I had it happen one time without even realizing it. A hive got mean for no apparent reason, then nice again three weeks later. We figured it out-- we must have accidently killed the queen, and they re-queened themselves. It probably happens more than we realize if we don't have marked queens and locate them regularly. I think it disturbs the hive too much to actually locate the queen, unless she just happens to be up where you are working. She can be; you never know what a queen will do. They don't always read the beekeeping books. Because of that, always be very careful when removing frames or working the hive. When removing frames, start with one of the edge frames and remove it to make more room to work. Try to work hives in warm weather so the propolis is soft and doesn't make the frames or boxes pop out with a jerk. Move slowly and gently when removing boxes. Set them on an upturned top cover so there is space under the box so you don't accidentally smash the queen if she is there, or lose her in the grass. One beekeeper friend of mine found his marked queen once – on the bottom of his shoe – not where you want to find your queen. Assume she could be on any frame you handle, even a honey frame, although if it is fully capped that is unlikely. Along with being careful to prevent the beekeeper from killing the queen (probably the biggest source of queen mortality), you want to look for signs of her presence or absence. If you find eggs or larva three days old or younger, she is probably there. If you go back a week later and only find capped brood, that is bad. It takes ten days to cap brood. If there is no open brood, only capped brood, she has been gone for a week to ten days, or more.

If a hive is queen-rite, it will act "normal", meaning that when you open the hive, the bees are working in an organized fashion and hardly notice you are there. However, a queenless hive will often be grumpy and aggressive. When you open the cover they will be just roaming around in a disorganized fashion and may fly up at you aggressively. Not all bees are aggressive when queenless, but many are. When the honey flow is on, the bees may or may not continue to collect honey if the queen is gone, so that is not a good indicator. Eventually the hive population will dwindle. If the queen died and there were no young eggs or brood to make into a queen, or even if there were and they panic and want a queen now, workers may begin to lay eggs. Because the workers are not fertile, these will be all drones. You will start to see lots of drone brood in a scattered pattern in the hive. Then there will be a lot of drones, too many, in the hive. Then you will start to see robbers, both bees from other hives and yellow jackets and bumblebees enter the hive and not be challenged. If you ever see yellow jackets in the hive who are not being challenged, that hive is in serious trouble. This is the hive that will show signs of varroa mite infestation. If you have a screened bottom board, you will find dead mites. If you remove drone larva it will have mites on it. You may see mites on adult bees. The hive may be too far gone at this point to help it. If it is late in the season, it is probably too late to re-queen and it will have to be counted a loss. This is a prime example of how the mites are just a symptom of a weak hive. They are always out there waiting to move in, but a strong, healthy hive will keep them out. A weak, helpless hive will be overcome. To let it go is a probably the best thing to do because unless the beekeeper killed the queen, the hive had some intrinsic problem that you don't want propagated. It sounds cruel, but in nature the fittest survive and the weak die and that is how survivor organisms emerge.

Chapter 9
Honey Management

I already discussed how we collect honey. After we collect the honey we store it in our warm garage. Make sure all doors and windows have screens or are closed because the bees will find the honey and you will have a room full of bees. We had a situation where we had a garage sale in the fall and left the doors of the garage open and all the empty beehive boxes stacked on a shelf. The bees came, the customers left, and we ended up with piles of dead bees on the floor where they had fought over the honey supers. It was a mess, to say the least. Keep the doors and windows closed! For extracting, we like to choose a nice hot summer day so the honey flows well. We set up a table to uncap and make an assembly line. One person uncaps, one extracts, one bottles if we do it all at once. We have a hand-crank extractor. It has the capability to extract tangentially or radially, but after experimentation, we feel it empties the frames

better tangentially, even though we have to stop and turn the frames around once. It is also easier on the foundationless frames because the side of the basket supports the frame. Because we hand crank, we can control the force. We start slowly and gradually increase speed, then reverse the process to slow down,

Frames in extractor

especially with the foundationless frames. Although we are not always so careful, we have very few blow outs, especially with older comb and medium frames. If we do have a blow out, we just fish out the comb and crush and strain it in a filter placed over a bucket. We make decisions about what to extract, what to use as cut comb and what to crush and strain. If we have really messed up comb, we will harvest it to get it out of the hive and crush and strain, or use part of it for cut comb if there is a big enough part that is nice enough for that.

In every state there are specific laws for bottling, labeling and selling honey. Make sure you are aware of the laws in your state if you would like to sell honey. Many small beekeepers just use their own honey and give it away to friends and family. Some states even frown on that without following their guidelines, but most would not do anything to you for giving your great-aunt a jar of honey. However, if you decide to sell, even from your home, the regulations can vary from none at all to having to have a state-approved honey house, depending on the state. Educate yourself on your state's laws. Contact your state bee association for that information.

You can buy honey bottles and labels from any bee supplier. You can also use canning jars and make your own labels. Just make sure the labels comply with the state's requirements. Honey is a naturally preserved product, but it will crystallize, especially in cool temperatures. We find it is best to bottle any honey you want to bottle soon after extraction. Summer honeys crystallize more slowly than fall honeys, but all honey bottles easiest when it is freshly extracted. We extract into a strainer bucket, which can be used for a bottling bucket directly afterwards. If we can't bottle immediately, we store the honey in the bucket until we can. If it is later in the season, don't leave a bucket of honey in an unheated area overnight. We ended up with an entire bucket of creamed honey one year by doing that.

Think about what your ultimate goal is for your honey. We like to keep at least two or three five gallon buckets back for our own use. We don't bother to bottle that, because we use it right out of the bucket. We don't start bottling for sale until we have reached our quota for our personal use. Over the years I have experimented with all types of jars and bottles and finally settled on three sizes – quarts, pints and one pound jars. These are what most people who buy my honey seem to want. I gravitated toward glass because it is easier to re-use and looks nicer. I also gravitated toward wider mouthed jars because it is easier to get crystallized honey out of a wide mouth jar.

If a customer brings me a clean jar, I give them a dollar off the jar of honey. That way my jars get recycled. These are just practical things I developed to make life easier for me. Over time a pattern will develop for how your honey gets used/distributed. Don't waste time and packaging for things that will just set on a shelf and gather dust. Figure out who likes what and what you actually sell or give away and do what works best for that. Make life as simple and easy on yourself as you can so that you can make the best use of your time and resources. I experimented with a lot of different types of packaging and types of honey (comb honey, creamed honey, liquid honey) and over time settled on either what sells or what I can use myself if it doesn't sell.

Cutting Comb Honey

Bottled honey

Do also be aware of your state's food laws. In some states flavors and additives can be legally added to honey without a commercial kitchen, but in others only pure honey can be sold without special facilities and licensing. We once had an out of state speaker come to a local bee club meeting and give us great ideas for how to sell value-added honey products. Unfortunately most of what he suggested was illegal in our state. He had no idea because it was legal in his state. If you read or hear a good suggestion, check it out before investing a lot of time and resources to make something you can't sell. At the very least, make sure if you are experimenting that it is something you will use yourself if you can't sell it legally, or if no one wants to buy it. I personally like to try to make whatever I can myself. It is a personal challenge for me to try to produce things others just go to the store and buy. Because of this perverse nature of mine, I have developed lip balm, lotions, soaps, lotion bars, bar-b-que sauce, ketchup, honey sweetened jams and jellies and every manner of baked good that would normally be made with sugar, made with honey. All of this was developed for personal use by myself and my family. Some things can be sold legally, like the lip balm and soap and lotions. Our state does not allow any processed foods other than non-perishable baked goods and jams and jellies to be sold without a commercial kitchen and a food handling license. I don't worry about it because my main goal is to produce for my own use and if I have the good fortune of having excess, then I sell it. Pure, liquid honey sells the best anyway. The public is getting increasingly educated on the value of pure, local foods and the demand is growing. I usually don't have enough to supply what is asked of me.

This brings up another important question. How much should you charge for your honey? The big answer to that is "it depends". Mostly it depends on who your market is. Do some market research. Find out what other beekeepers in your area are charging. Go to local farmer's markets. This is a little hard, I have found. Farmer's markets only a few miles apart can have very different clientele. You don't want to underprice your honey and undercut the market for other local beekeepers, but you don't want to overprice it, either. You are not in competition with other local beekeepers, you are in this together. You need to make it clear to the public that pure, local honey is a valuable product and is worth a decent asking price. However, if you price it above what other local beekeepers are asking, you won't sell any. No matter how much excess honey you produce, you probably will have a strong market to sell it. This is why you should not see your fellow beekeeper as competition. Another consideration in your pricing is the size of your operation. If you have five or less hives and just five gallons of excess honey to sell for the whole season, it is reasonable that you will have to charge more to make it worth your while to package and label the honey. Make sure you cover your costs for packaging and labeling in your price. Remember that printer ink and label stock are not free, so if you are printing your own labels, it may actually cost you more than buying labels from a honey supplier. I found this was true for myself. I had an owner of a local confection company ask about reselling my honey in his store. I gave him my "resale" prices, since I am a small bee-keeper and don't have enough honey to "wholesale". He asked, legitimately, why he could buy honey from a commercial beekeeper for half of my prices. I explained it was a matter of scale. I really didn't have enough honey to supply him anyway.

Chapter 10
But what about the mites?

Of course, scale brings up other concerns. As I have mentioned over and over, larger producers find the need to use chemical controls and there is more of a concern with contamination in the honey. All miticides have usage instructions, required by law. Humans tend to ignore such things and don't always follow the labels, or the laws. My state doesn't have a functional apiary inspection program, for good or bad, so there is no one to be sure these laws are followed except the individual beekeeper. Even if the labels are followed precisely, I am not convinced that contamination is eliminated. For instance, miticides are not supposed to be placed during honey flow. Beekeepers interpret this (and rightly so I believe) to mean strictly when honey supers are on the hive. So, I have read accounts of beekeepers who treat for mites in early spring when they consider all the boxes on the hive to be strictly brood boxes. This is more easily defined for most commercial beekeepers because they use deep boxes exclusively for brood and shallow boxes exclusively for honey. They also always use queen excluders when they have honey supers on, so there is no brood in the honey supers. They pull the mite strips, or whatever treatment they used, when they add honey supers in early summer. They then remove the supers in mid- summer when many areas experience a mild dearth. During this period many will again apply mite treatments to the hives. They then remove these in time for a fall honey flow and put on honey supers to collect that. After the fall flow is finished, they remove the honey supers and again treat for mites to theoretically bring the numbers down to an acceptable level for successful overwintering. I personally am not convinced that there are always true "dearths" every year in every situation. My climate is extremely variable and I think my bees are bringing in honey most of the warm season, except on days they can't fly. So, theoretically if I have taken off all my honey supers, they are storing this honey in the brood chambers, which are being treated for mites in these commercial hives. When the honey supers are put back on with the queen excluders in place, the bees say, "Good! Now we can make more room for the queen to lay by moving this honey out of the brood nest and up into the honey supers!" Do you see the problem? The honey stored in the brood nest has been exposed to the mite treatments. To make more room for brood nest expansion during the next honey flow, any extra honey stored down there will get moved up into the honey supers. This is why I think no mite treatment is safe and any hive treated with it has potentially contaminated honey. I don't discourage customers from buying from larger beekeepers, I just educate them and give them information so they can ask informed questions when considering whether or not to purchase honey from a particular producer.

Most "experts" will say this is just a necessary evil and that without the use of mite controls, all hives will die. They feel that the contamination possibility is very small, so it is a risk that is acceptable. Long-time beekeepers who kept bees before the varroa crisis hit in the 1980's have an interesting perspective on this situation. Prior to the emergence of the varroa mite on the beekeeping scene, beekeepers were fighting pesticides and pushing for the banning of those that were the most toxic. This is because millions of honeybees were being killed off by incorrectly applied pesticides or over-sprays. The beekeepers were successful, especially because there was an increased awareness of how these things were causing a disruption in the environment which was highlighted by people like Rachel Carson in her book "Silent Spring". When hives suddenly began to die off because of the varroa mite, beekeepers did a 180 degree turn and started begging the government to bring back previously banned pesticides so they could use them IN THEIR HIVES to control the mites. Again, they were successful and they did exactly that. Some of these longer-term beekeepers are still scratching their heads trying to figure out why on earth beekeepers would do such a thing. Others just went with the flow and felt they had to do what was necessary to save their bees. Of course, over time the mites became resistant to those first miticides. It was then necessary to bring out other chemicals to use. Maybe it is their goal to breed a "super mite" that can live in the presence of any toxic chemical and without its host, the honeybee, since the bee is dead from the treatment that was given to "save" it. I tell people it is like this: If you had a rat hanging off your dog, would you feed the dog rat poison to kill the rat?

So, along with the potential honey contamination, we are adding a new factor now, the possibility that we are actually poisoning our own bees with the treatment we put on to "help" them. Bees and mites are too similar in make-up to use pesticides to kill one of them. A larger dose of the same chemicals caused millions of bees to die instantly. So, when the beekeepers scratch their heads and blame agricultural chemicals for the weakness of the bee population and hive die offs, perhaps they are overlooking a huge possibility. It's the proverbial elephant in the middle of the room that no one quite wants to admit is there, so they just pretend it doesn't exist. It seems like common sense to me that if the beekeeper must wear a ventilator and protective gear to just apply some of these things and then place a warning sign in his or her apiary telling people to keep out until the treatment dissipates, perhaps this is not very good for the bees? Add to this the factors which affect the application of these chemicals, many of which are vapors that will vaporize at different temperatures and humidity conditions. In my region we joke that if you don't like the weather, wait ten minutes and it will change. How can you be sure the chemical is vaporizing at the rate the scientist calculated in his controlled laboratory setting? I have also heard people say a chemical is safe if it is natural or naturally derived. Well, I have two things to say about that. First, poison hemlock is natural. Second, when I was a brand-new beekeeper, on the advice of a friend I put some peppermint essential oil on the bottom board of my hive to help with natural mite control. He told me to mix it with baby oil, put some on a paper towel and place the paper towel on the bottom board of the hive. Misunderstanding his directions, I completely soaked the paper towel and placed it on the bottom board. Almost immediately the entire hive vacated the premises. He had a good laugh and then explained he meant just a small amount on the paper towel. If a little is good a lot is better, right? It's all natural, right? I think you see my point.

But wait! We are in the scientific age, right? Can't we control all nature with science? Well, it appears there are two opinions about that. The one is yes, we can, and because we can the world is getting better and better. Someday all people will be rich and well fed and live in an industrialized world where all food is produced through the latest scientific processes and everyone will be happy and not have to work hard to do anything. The other opinion is that the industrialized system is already broke and we are just starting to realize the tip of the iceberg of how bad it is and how bad it will get if something better isn't put in its place. In the group with this second opinion, there is much variability about what exactly is wrong and how exactly to fix it. I personally am of the opinion that nature has been chugging along quite well for thousands of years. Suddenly around 150 – 200 years ago we decided that machines and science could do it better than nature. This idea grew slowly at first, but gained momentum, especially in the 20th century, when large scale wars prompted us to accelerate the pace of science and industry. Just like anything when it is new, this produced an amazing prosperity and apparent higher standard of living for those privileged to live in the industrialized world. But one of the laws of thermodynamics states that we are in a closed system and that nothing really changes, it just gets redistributed. So, if one part of the world suddenly starts living like kings, other parts of the world have to move to a lower standard than they once had to accommodate it. Apparently there are only so many resources available and if part of the population has more than its share, the rest have less than their share. No, I am not in favor of redistribution, I just think that maybe we have gone a little too far in trying to get away from our natural roots. This has created unintended consequences. Now, to fix the apparent disparity we try to come up with more of the same things that caused it in the first place. I just want to put on the brakes, back up a little bit, look critically at where we are and re-evaluate and see if perhaps we can find a better, simpler way without getting too radical.

Nature seems to have its own ability to achieve balance. If left to itself it seems to eventually regain a balance even where a very apparent imbalance occurred before. I was told by a beekeeper/researcher that he had traveled to South Africa during the height of the varroa crisis. The beekeepers there did not have the resources to treat their hives for the varroa mite, so they just let nature take its course. In four years' time a balance was regained and varroa was no longer an issue for those beekeepers. I am sure it was a hardship for a period of time for those beekeepers. I am sure they took a financial hit. However, if we were to add up all the money and time that has been spent on varroa mite control and research it would be far more than the commercial beekeepers (or any beekeepers) would lose in four years' time here in the U.S. Benjamin Franklin said an ounce of prevention is worth a pound of cure. If we really want to make beekeeping financially profitable, perhaps we should think of the prevention side rather than just wasting millions of dollars a year to fight a losing battle with the mites. For some reason we just can't take that step. It seems too risky. We will try new treatments that are untested, or even try chemicals off label that we have no idea what they will do, but we won't even entertain the idea of building up the hives and letting them fight their own battles instead. I guess it is a control issue. I am willing to let the bees do the hard work and be their own boss, so I can do more other things. I am not a full-time beekeeper. I have other interests, mostly in agriculture. During most of the beekeeping season those things require more of my intense consideration than the bees do. The bees clean their own house, make their own food and birth and raise their own babies. I don't have to plant them, water them, transplant them or weed them. I try to only open the hives once a month except in spring build-up or strong honey flow. This allows me to keep enough of an eye on them so I can intervene if a serious problem occurs, but gives them enough space to do what they do best – make honey. Many times they solve their own problems without my intervention. I believe this produces stronger, healthier bees that can survive over a long period of time. This approach will seem too radical to many people. So be it, I am just offering another option in the sea of bee-keeping opinion. What each one does with it is up to him or her.

Chapter 11
Late Season Management

Sorry for the soapbox interruption. I put the varroa discussion in-between mid and late season management because that is where, as I stated above, those that treat will place treatments and will again place them in the fall. So, if you choose to try to manage hives without those treatments, you need to be aware of what those who question your sanity are talking about. Long term hive health is something you are always trying to achieve and you do that by making sure first and foremost that the bees are adequately fed. If you want them to have the best food so they can be as strong and healthy as possible, you want to leave enough honey on the hive for them to successfully overwinter. They worked hard to collect and evaporate that honey. Their goal was to make enough to survive the winter. If you take too much and then give them back sugar water, you are short-circuiting the whole process. Your goal is to breed better bees that can take care of themselves. If you take all their hard work and replace it with an inferior feed, you are making them weak and dependent and making all the effort on their part and yours wasted. Like I stated before, bees are wild creatures, not domesticated animals. They know exactly what food is good for them and they gather it better than any human ever could. I have heard experts say that the fall honey isn't best for the bees because it crystalizes too quickly. If this is true, why do they collect that honey in the fall? Or why do those flowers bloom in the fall? Why has it worked for hundreds/thousands of years if it isn't the best thing for the bees? Maybe they do know better than I do, and I should just get out of their way and let them work. In my area fall honey is goldenrod. It is very pungent, both in and out of the hive, and crystalizes very quickly. It really isn't the best honey for human consumption anyway, so why not let the bees have it? I try to not collect any honey after the first of September. Our average first frost is the first week of October. I figure that gives the bees a whole month to fill a super for winter. Remember that all summer long I left a full extra box of honey on the hive, which I did not touch. That was my insurance. I then let them make another full box. Some years they are able to make it, others they are not. Because I left that box on earlier in the season, I rarely have to supplementary feed my bees in the fall.

So how much honey do you need to leave on the hive? This is the million dollar question. I leave the super I had on all summer plus the one they hopefully filled in the fall. I also assume that they have filled the brood box with honey, or even "heft" the hive to see how heavy it is. In recent years I have worried less about this, because they seem to do it. Some people feed sugar water also and even put in candy boards for insurance. If you have left plenty of honey, there is no harm in doing that if it makes you feel better. Just don't do it as a substitute for honey. I also believe whatever you do for feed, do it in the fall before it gets really cold. I personally do not believe in lifting the lid of the hive, even the top cover, if the temperature is below 55 or 60 degrees. I don't think it is wise to do that even to refill a feeder or place a candy board. I think the bees have a way of establishing an equilibrium in the hive over the winter and if you disturb it, you could kill them. I know others have done it routinely for years and have gotten away with it, but I feel it is better to be safe than sorry. Many people will recommend that you feed in the late winter/early spring when the weather gets fitful and the bees move up into the top box of the hive. The theory is that if the bees are in the top box, they are at the end of their stores and ready to starve out and die. This theory believes that bees will never go back down, only up. It also believes that the bees always do exactly what the books say they will do. I decided what I don't know won't hurt me. I don't check. They don't tell. If I had a strong hive with enough honey, they usually survive, regardless. I have also always read that bees live and die as a colony. If you find a dead cluster, the hive is dead. Well, one year I had two hives with a dead cluster and a live cluster. It had been the coldest February on record, and I think the outside of the cluster got too cold and died, but the inside survived and moved on when the weather mitigated. In both hives the dead cluster was toward the entrance and the live cluster further into the honey stores. A friend also had the same situation the same winter.

My two hives were in different locations in two different hive styles, so I know it wasn't the location or the hive style that caused it.

This brings up the next issue with preparing the hives in the fall. Like I said, I stop all honey collection after the last of August. During September I check for hive health. I want to see evidence that the queen is still laying. I want to see busy activity at the entrances. I begin to think about winter configuration. Whatever the configuration, I have come to the conclusion that at least for me in my region, wrapping my hives for winter is an advantage. Because of that, I have to make sure that my hives are in a configuration that will allow for proper ventilation with the winter wrap on. I don't put the wrap on until October, but since the weather in October is unpredictable, I don't want to be moving hive bodies around, or even popping lids and inner covers if it is too cold. Sometimes it is sunny and 70 degrees, sometimes rainy and 40, you never know in October. What I want for a hive configuration going into winter is a minimum of four medium boxes, the top one full of honey, no partial frames. Most hives end up with five boxes. Occasionally I have a smaller hive, but if I feel it is heavy enough and has enough honey, I will prepare it anyway. If I need to rob from a stronger hive to help a weaker one I will do it at this point, but I try not to. Again, my goal is to get hives that can survive on their own. I also have horizontal configurations, but I will cover that in a separate chapter. Everything about them is simpler. I will just cover traditional vertical hives here. My inner covers have notches in them which all summer long have been turned so that the bees must enter through the inner cover hole to get into the hive. It is

Inner cover holes down for direct access to hive	Inner cover holes up for access only through center hole

easier for the bees to guard the hole this way. With winter approaching, I flip them so that they may enter directly to the frames from the notch. The reason for this is that I like to put an insulating/absorbing blanket in the space between the inner cover and the top cover, which is created by my 3" spacer. If I don't flip the inner cover my blanket will block the inner cover hole and they won't be able to use the top entrance. Use of the top entrance is critical in winter, when the bottom entrance gets blocked by snow and ice. It is also critical for upper ventilation, and if it is blocked, it cannot work for that purpose. I flip this while the weather is still warm, so I don't have to disturb the hive on a cold day when I am ready to install the blanket. Usually it is well glued by propolis, and the colder it is, the harder it

Reduced entrance on long hive in winter

is to pry it off and the more it disrupts the bees.

For September that is sufficient. If somehow I find a queenless hive, I let it go. I do not believe in combining strong and weak hives. In my experience it only makes another weak hive and it dies anyway. When October comes, I place a wooden entrance reducer in the entrance on the "summer" setting, which is the wider setting. This is small enough to keep out mice, but large enough to allow ventilation and the exit of dead bees if the weather cooperates enough for house cleaning. In the past I just stapled ½" hardware cloth over the opening, leaving it fully open. I still don't think that is a bad idea, it's just easier to slide in the entrance reducer (usually), than to staple on the hardware cloth. I then cut and fit one layer of Reflectix bubble wrap insulation around the hive and staple it on with a staple gun. I use the longest staples I can find – 9/16". In the spring I carefully remove this and re-use it until it is shredded, so it can be re-used for several seasons. Because this is silver and reflective, it needs something on the outside both for the bees and the beekeeper. It is positively

Insulating Hive

Insulated hives in snow

blinding in the sun! So, I cut and wrap one layer of black tar paper, which can also be re-used for several seasons with care, over the Reflectix, also stapled on with a staple gun. I make sure the inner cover holes and the lower entrance holes are free and clear so the bees can come and go and there is proper ventilation. Some of my inner covers have extra notches we added for ventilation. The bees usually propolize them until only one is open anyway, so I think the single notch is sufficient, although sometimes I get a little mold with only one, so to be safe make at least one extra on the back side of the inner cover. I then pop a blanket, or alternately, a burlap bag with a raw sheep fleece in it, under the top cover and we are ready for winter. It literally takes five to ten minutes per hive, especially if the materials are re-used and pre-cut.

The blankets are nothing special. I found $2 blankets at the local Salvation Army Store and keep them for that purpose. The blankets serve to insulate and also absorb excess moisture in the top.

Not everyone insulates. I did not most of my beekeeping career. I started in earnest only after losing all my hives in the worst winter in 25 years. The only people who had hives survive that year were those who had insulated their hives. I

Placing blanket in spacer under top cover

had tried tar paper in the past and it seemed to make no difference, so I concluded that in our region it was unnecessary. Now I have modified my opinion. We are in the gray area. At 45 degrees latitude and farther north it is necessary to insulate every winter. At 40 degrees latitude and farther south, it is not necessary. We are at 43 degrees latitude. Since we usually have a roller coaster weather pattern in the winter, from sub- zero to above freezing in the space of a week on a regular basis, I think the insulation helps to keep the hive more moderate. This makes it less stressful for the bees. One winter we had the coldest February on record. When it gets so cold the cluster cannot move, it will eventually starve if the weather doesn't moderate. We had five weeks when it was that cold. That was when I had the dead and live clusters in the same hive. My friend with the same situation had also insulated. I think if our hives had not been insulated we would just have had a dead-out. I believe the insulation gave them just enough of an edge to be able to move out to the honey stores. I went a lot of years without doing it. Now I think I will always do it. It doesn't matter what you use to insulate. One woman in our bee club just wrapped old carpet around her hive, but it survived. It doesn't have to be pretty. I do think the easier it is, the more likely you will do it. I do think it has helped my winter survival. It went from an average of 50% survival up to 80% survival last winter and I think the 20% that died had other issues. One of those was wind. I had not protected one of my hive sites sufficiently from the prevailing winter winds. The most exposed hive died. I have corrected that now – time will tell how it changes my overwintering success. The other hive that died I believe was either very weak or possibly queenless going into winter. That was another situation of too much beekeeper intervention. I felt I should mark my queens in the apiary I use for teaching. I have never done it, so I am not skilled. I accidentally totally covered the queen with paint. I don't know if I killed her, or maimed her or what, but that hive certainly wasn't as strong after that point. I decided that it is not a good idea to mark queens. If you buy a new package or nucleus hive and she is already marked, fine, but it is not worth killing her to mark her yourself, unless you are skilled, or must know for breeding purposes how old your queen is.

I briefly mentioned wind breaks. You need to protect your hives from strong winds, especially the prevailing winter winds. Some beekeepers use temporary windbreaks just for the winter. There are a lot of options. The best is to place your hives in a place with a natural windbreak. One of my hive locations is in front of a wooded area. The woods act as a natural wind-

Windbreak fence behind hives in field

break. Another location is in a gravel pit with a berm. The hives sit nice and cozy behind that where they are protected. However I have another location in the middle of a hay field that is open and exposed. There is a world of difference between these locations on a windy spring day. I cannot even open the hives in the open field, but the others are fine when it is a warm sunny spring day with a strong wind. I have put up semi-temporary wind breaks around the hives in the field. One beekeeper friend put up a year-round open fence and covered it with used billboard ads that he obtained through some means unknown to me. Since they were designed for all weather, they stood up to strong winter winds. He takes them down for the summer. Sometimes he puts them inside out, sometimes he lets the ads be displayed. Other friends like to find similar uses for old political signs... Planting a hedge to create a new natural windbreak is also an option. Just make sure it is a hardy plant that can handle the winds as well.

Insulated, ventilated hive with natural windbreak.

By the beginning of November, all winter preparations should be complete. Windbreaks should be up, insulation on and any absorbing blankets you may want to use in place. Ventilation is very important all year 'round in the beehive, but in the winter it can make the difference between survival and death. Make sure there is an upper entrance of some type that can be used by the bees for winter cleansing flights and also for warm, moist air to escape. A blanket, wood chips or other natural absorbent material can be used to help absorb excess moisture. I am not sure this is absolutely necessary, but it doesn't hurt, so why not? You don't have to buy expensive manufactured equipment for this, though. Just keep it simple. I keep my 3" spacers on my hive all year long and just put a blanket in there in the winter. When I remember…

Now you can take time to evaluate your beekeeping year. Decide if there are any major management changes you want for next year. Clean and properly store your empty equipment and tools. I know storage can be an issue. If you want to keep wax moths out of unused equipment with drawn comb, keep it in a place that will freeze in the winter. Try to cover any openings with tape or by using a cover. Try not to store drawn comb by gasoline or equipment that has gasoline in it – the fumes are toxic. One beekeeper friend of mine hangs his empty boxes from a long board in the ceiling of his barn. They are up and out of the way, but he can see what he has when he needs it. Evaluate what you might need for the next beekeeping season and make plans to buy or build it. Decide what to do about bees. If only half your hives make it, can you get by without buying bees? If you answer yes – keeping in mind you should be able to make at least one split from each overwintered hive – take the chance and don't order bees. If you feel that won't work (maybe you only have one hive, for instance) make plans to order bees – preferably a local nuc from someone you trust to be a good beekeeper. Make arrangements early because reputable bee sellers sell out quickly.

As winter settles in, resist the urge to check on the bees except from the outside. Check from the outside as often as you like, but please don't lift that lid! If you get a nice pleasant sunny day at or above freezing, especially after a cold stretch, you should see signs that the bees have been out on cleansing flights. You may see dead bees in the snow or bee droppings in the snow or around the entrance. You will be able to tell what they are using for an entrance this way. Don't worry about clearing the bottom entrance unless it makes you feel better. As long as the upper entrance is free and clear, the bees will be OK. I know beekeepers who go away for the whole winter to warmer, sunnier climates and their bees survive the winter just fine. It is interesting to watch and observe and learn what the bees do in winter, but they really do best left to themselves. Some people listen with a stethoscope or their ear pressed to the side of the hive to see if they hear the cluster buzzing. I have heard this may not be the best thing after all, because winter hardy bees in cold regions seem to do best and consume the least stores when they are quiet and less active. I don't listen. Occasionally I have had one of my kids listen for me, but it rarely gives me much information that means anything by spring. Some beekeepers use heat sensors to determine if the cluster is alive. If it makes you happy to spend money that way, go for it. If it is dead, there isn't much you can do anyway. I am skeptical of beekeepers who tell me in January or February that they have X number of dead hives. I think it is impossible to tell if they are alive or dead at that point. I would not take down a presumed dead hive in mid-winter. You could be killing your best hive that just has learned how to best conserve stores for the long haul. If you are tempted, just don't go out there. Leave them alone and let spring tell you the story.

So, what defines spring? As I said before, I will not open a hive until the daffodils bloom. I learned my lesson the hard way my first over-wintered spring. It was March, one of those beautiful 70 degree days we get some years. There was grass, warm sunshine-- surely the bees were ready to come out, right? Being a novice, I didn't realize it was too early for capped brood. I opened the hives and saw what looked like empty frames. I spread them out on the grass, assuming the hives were dead. I did this to three hives. Then I left them that way and went to check another hive across the street. As I was checking that one, my daughter suddenly spotted eggs – lots of eggs, whole frames of eggs. Oh boy, maybe those other hives were in the same condition! We rushed back, checked and sure enough we had left frames full of eggs exposed for almost an hour. We put them back together, but alas, it was too late and we learned a hard lesson that day. We killed three really strong hives by being too hasty. After that lesson, I have never opened my hives until the daffodils bloom, even if it is almost the end of April. Seasons come and go and no two years are the same. To mark a date on the calendar would only lead to success about half the time, and disaster the rest. Many people will feed sugar water in the early spring to make sure the bees make it to first nectar. I am trying to breed self-sufficient bees, so I don't do this. I suspect bees are finding something to bring in long before I see any signs of spring. My hives are all near wooded areas. I know there are willows and other native plants that send out pollen very early. I have read that if bees are low on honey they won't collect pollen, but I see bees laden with pollen one after the other coming into the hives when there seems to be nothing at all blooming. At any rate, I decide to leave them alone and let them sort it out.

When that day comes and it is over 55 degrees and the daffodils are blooming, I take off the winter wrap and open the hives. Usually I find the whole hive full of bees, but sometimes the top box is empty. I lift it off and go on down. If no one greets me at this point, I begin to think the hive is dead. I am looking for a dead cluster and thinking of what was the cause. If I don't find a dead cluster yet, I keep look-ing. If the hive is dead, eventually I will find the dead cluster. I pull the hive apart, clean up the equipment and take it away for storage. All the while I am looking for clues to its demise. If it is completely empty of honey, I know they starved out. Although after my first season or two this has not happened. Usually these dead-outs will have a whole box of honey left on them, or even two boxes. If I find dead drones on the bottom board, I will assume they were queenless going into winter. If I find a significant number of dead yellow jackets in the pile on the bottom board, I will assume either they were queenless, or perhaps the yellow jackets aided in their demise. I am not entirely convinced yellow jackets can't take over a weak hive in the fall, kill the queen and effectively kill the hive. Sometimes there are just too many dead yellow jackets on the bottom board for me to think otherwise. If there is a lot of mold in the hive, they may have gotten too wet and chilled and died. Sometimes you just never know what happened. If, however the hive is alive, usually they will have done most of the housekeeping before I got there. I will go through the hive to the bottom and even clean off the bottom board if necessary, but usually it is not necessary; the bees have already taken care of that. I remove any entrance reducers at this point. When I put the hive back together, I try to take out any boxes that are completely empty, but be very careful about this-- they could have eggs, remember? Check very well before removing boxes. Once I removed an empty box, and in my hurry, left it outside the hive, covered, so any bees that hadn't left could exit before removing it. Coming back a few days later, I discovered the queen was in that box! She was alive and well, but just think if I had taken it away! After putting the hive back together, I turn the inner cover back over so they have to use the inner cover hole to get in, and I do not replace the blanket I had for winter. If all was well, that blanket is dry. Occasionally I have had a leaky roof or other problem and had a wet blanket. This is fortunate, because the moisture didn't go into the hive, it was absorbed by the blanket. I evaluate the cause and correct it, if this happens.

The last step is to properly store your winter wrap and blankets so they can be used next season. The blankets need to be put in a place where mice won't make nice homes in them and destroy them over the summer. Make sure they are dry before storage or they will mildew and be useless the next fall. If you are careful when removing the wraps, you can re-use them several times. Don't worry about staples left in the hives. Now that the weather is nice, re-paint any equipment that needs painting so you are ready for those splits and swarms that will be coming in the next month or so. If you have new bees coming, get equipment ready for them. If the weather is nice, paint outside to keep the mess to a minimum and so the paint will dry faster. Also remember to record the condition of each hive you opened. This will be very important in the coming weeks. This is the time of year to keep a close watch on the hives. They will build up fast and the window for splits and swarms may be very small, so you need to be ready, both with your equipment and your schedule.

Chapter 12
What kind of bees?

When I first started beekeeping I had already been keeping livestock for a short time. In my preparations for keeping livestock, I had carefully studied the different breeds and then determined what breed(s) would suit my environment and management style. So, naturally I thought beekeeping would be similar. When I ordered my first packages of bees, I asked the seller, "What type of bees will these be?" There was a pause on the other end of the phone, then he said, "Well, they are Italians." He meant, what else would they be? My bee books had mentioned several "races" of bees, which I interpreted to mean "breeds" like the livestock, and that beekeepers raised different ones just like livestock producers did. In reality, most beekeepers kept Italian bees at that time. Some experimented with others, but for the vast majority, Italians were it. No one questioned it, and most bee literature assumed you would be raising Italians. So, Italians it was. The first few years they did well. Then I propagated a local swarm's offspring for several seasons. Each year the progeny got meaner and meaner. It got to where my daughter and I dreaded working the bees. Even with a good smoker going full bore, we were getting stung through our bee suits. She took to wearing jeans under her bee suit in even the hottest weather. In the fourth winter, which was quite mild by our region's standards, they all died. They died in the top super with a full super of honey underneath. One hive just forgot to cluster and died all over the hive. Enough was enough. I decided to try something new. I ordered Carniolans from northern California. They were certified disease free and non-Africanized. I had read they wintered in smaller clusters, requiring less honey. I had also read they reacted better to the rise and fall of the nectar flows, so they were overall more hardy. Apparently they also have a nice, gentle disposition. I have been very pleased with this choice and won't go back. I do have Italians mixed in, because the queens mate with both kinds of drones. However, my drones are Carniolan and as each year goes by, my hives get darker and darker and more of my home-grown queens are dark instead of golden. This is my story and I know others have their own favorite "race" of bee. Ultimately the best bee is the one adapted to your environment. I like them to be nice, too. Some people think getting stung is a rite of passage and angry bees are better for some reason, but I get plenty of honey and enjoy it so much more with nice bees. I rarely use my smoker, though I always have it ready. I feel that any bees of any race that are coming from a known Africanized region will have the potential for a nasty disposition.

I do not suggest that you spend lots of money on a special queen of a particular breed. This is often done. In fact, our local bee club went to great lengths to get a large number of queens from Canada to jump start the local beekeepers. The problem was that most of us weren't the best at introducing a new queen to the hive. I know the $45 queen I attempted to introduce was killed by the hive I tried to introduce her to. I later figured out how to do it better, but it was too late in the season anyway, and I am sure she would have perished regardless. It is expensive and risky to go that route. Besides, if you decide to raise your own replacement queens as I do, the first generation will mate with 21 or so drones hanging around, and there go your special genetics you spent the big bucks for. Remember that queens have to open mate, and there probably aren't a lot of drones of that type around unless other beekeepers in the area are also raising that breed of bee. So, start with what you can find locally.

Livestock breeders like purebred animals for a number of reasons. I like to cross-breed because I get a deeper gene pool that way. Bees are no different, except that they are even more susceptible to genetic narrowing than most livestock, so diversity is even more important. Like I said before, the best bee is the one adapted to your region. There are bee breeders who have been working on breeding adapted bees in each region. They are out there. Ask around and you may find them. If you have to drive a couple of hours to get a good nucleus hive for your "foundation stock", that is fine. Better to start out with good, strong stock than to waste the same amount of money on something that will die over winter with or without giving you any honey in the meantime. When I sell livestock, I like the buyer to come out and visit so I can educate them on proper management. As a bee buyer, you should do the same. Try to go to where the bees are being raised. Observe the operation and the beekeeper. Is it well managed and clean? Does the beekeeper seem to know what he/she is doing? Have they managed for disease and know that their hives are strong and healthy? Are the queens local or from out of state/region? Most importantly, can you inspect the nucleus hive (nuc) before you buy it? I had some new beekeepers come to an educational field day who discovered after driving almost two hours one way to pick up two nucs that one of them did not have a queen. If the seller won't let you look, that is a red flag. In the best case scenario, the beekeeper will let you help make up the nuc. You bring a box to put the bees in. You help pull frames and find a queen, or transfer the competed nuc from the seller's box to yours. This gives you the chance to inspect each frame and to make sure there is a large, healthy queen in the hive and that she has brood. Hopefully you can get a peek at what her brood pattern looks like. It should be nice and tight, with few empty cells. It should cover most of the frame. You also need to make sure the comb looks clean and disease free. Educate yourself by looking in bee books to see what American Foul Brood, European Foul Brood, Nosema and Chalkbrood look like. Make sure the frames show no evidence of these or mold or wax moth damage.

If this sounds picky, good. I think beekeepers have been too lax about these things. They have relied on the chemical controls for disease and pests and have tolerated too low a standard for the bees themselves. Weak bees beget weak bees. Most packages and nucs will cost around the same amount regardless of where they come from. It isn't like livestock where some breeds are rarer and worth more money. A good livestock breeder can command a much higher price due to reputation. This isn't true of beekeepers. Mostly because the bees will breed in the open and that cannot be controlled, so with the exception of management for overall health, the beekeeper cannot really control how the bees turn out in a given generation. You can keep a small, strong and healthy nucleus hive strong and healthy with good management and a favorable location with good forage, but you cannot make a weak, sick hive healthy the same way. We need to get more selective so we have stronger, healthy survivor bees that can keep going year after year.

The last consideration is the queen. As I have stated, she should be local, not just put with local, overwintered bees. However, not all queens, local or not, are created equal. Good queen breeders will let the queen lay for a full two weeks prior to caging her or transferring her to another hive. If a queen is caged right after she is mated, or within just a few days, she will shut down laying. When she is released and re-starts, she may or may not continue to develop fully. If she does not, she will never be a good laying queen and will not lead a strong hive. If you are buying just a queen to start a hive or put with a split, ask about this. Queens caged too soon will not be good layers. Some beekeepers will sell virgin queens. I feel this is very risky. I know it can work because I have seen it work, but it seems the chances are about equal that it won't. The virgin queen doesn't smell like a real queen because she is not fully developed and fertile. The other bees don't recognize her as a queen. She is introduced like a regular queen. When she is released, presumably when she is accepted by the hive, then she must go on her mating flight. There is always the possibility a queen may not make it back from her mating flight, which is why in a normal situation there are multiple queen cells – just in case. The workers will guard at least one from the queen who emerged first, so they have insurance if she doesn't come back safely from her mating flight. With a single, introduced virgin queen, they don't have this insurance. Also, the virgin was not born in this hive, so she may or may not return to it following her mating flight. Since breeders will charge almost as much for a virgin as a mated queen, my recommendation is to buy only mated queens who have been caged after laying for a full two weeks' time. Another option is to buy ripe queen cells. This is fine if you don't have far to travel to move them into a queenless hive. Keep them warm, don't let them chill. Make sure you feel confident to place them in the hive. This takes a higher level of skill. I think there is a higher chance of acceptance by the bees because they will finish the cell and the queen will emerge in their hive, smelling like them. I personally let the bees raise their own queens as I have described earlier. This has been much simpler and I have had much more success than with trying to introduce queens.

Recently I have been selling frames of brood instead of finished nucs. We make sure there are young larva, eggs and capped brood. We notch some egg cells as we do for splits, then let the person take them home to raise the queen themselves. I sell them by the frame so it costs much less to the buyer and makes it much easier for me. I guarantee them a new frame of brood if they don't successfully raise a queen. I think this will help more people get started faster with locally adapted bees.

Chapter 13
Hive Designs

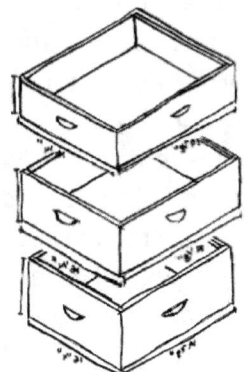

When I first started beekeeping everyone was using deep Langstroth hive bodies for the brood boxes, starting with one, then adding a second as the season went on. For honey supers most commercial beekeepers used a shallow – which is hardly used at all anymore. Hobby or smaller beekeepers used a medium super-- or some people called it an Illinois super-- for honey supers. I purchased all my boxes used from a long time beekeeper. He used deeps and mediums, so that is what I had. He also had a number of shallows and very shallow boxes used for cut-comb honey. He also had a few boxes designed and fitted with "Ross Rounds" a round comb honey system. This beekeeper, like many, was frugal with his resources, so he bought bulk

Langstroth Hive bodies—shallow, medium and deep boxes

materials from a number of different suppliers. Because I bought everything he had, there were boxes of frame parts and unused wax foundation. I have no idea how old the wax foundation was. There was no deep foundation, only medium and thin cut-comb foundation. There were no medium side bars, so I bought deep foundation and medium side bars to get started. I started with plastic foundation in my deep brood frames from the beginning. I used wax foundation in the mediums for honey supers until I ran out of medium foundation, then switched to plastic foundation. I have often wondered if the fact that I never really used much wax foundation contributed to never really having any varroa to speak of in my hives. I am sure other factors, especially good locations with lots of forage, also helped in that regard.

After a few years, the idea of using all mediums started to work its way around bee meetings. Being a small person with a similar small helper, this was appealing. We had been told early on that there were two kinds of beekeepers – those who had bad backs and those who will have bad backs. Not wanting to be one of those, we used team lifting and also moved full frames one by one into empty boxes to avoid lifting full deeps, which can weigh over a hundred pounds. Switching to all mediums helped with the weight issue, although they are still plenty heavy for one small person to lift. It also solved another problem we had. In the spring, the queen and all the bees had moved up into the honey supers and she had started laying a nice batch of brood in the medium frames. Now those frames were brood frames, so they weren't very pretty for honey frames, but also they were too shallow to put in the deep boxes with the rest of the brood frames. Using all one size box and frames allowed us to move those frames down into the brood boxes and if we wanted, nice full honey frames up to the honey supers from below. Since that time, eight frame mediums have been gaining some popularity for people not wanting the weight of ten frame boxes. It shaves around ten to fifteen pounds off the weight of a full box, which is very helpful, especially if the beekeeper is working alone.

General design of most top bar hives (without a stand)

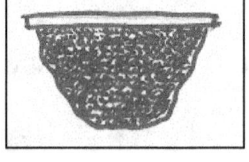

The lighter weight of the equipment certainly helped smaller and less strong beekeepers, but the boxes still had to be lifted and taken off to check down in the hive. Many beekeepers felt this was

Top bar with comb

not only hard on the beekeeper, but also on the bees. In the flurry of the "natural" beekeeping movement, many people became convinced that top bar hives were better for the bees. I had been doing field days for several years to help beekeepers, especially new beekeepers, learn what to do in their hives. A trend was developing where people were experimenting with both top bar and traditional hives.

The problem was that most of those trying the top bar hives were new beekeepers that hadn't figured out the best methods for keeping bees yet and they were experiencing a high rate of failure with the top bar hives. I decided that to help them achieve success, I should start a top bar hive myself to walk through the management and figure out how to make it work. I knew it could work because many people do manage them successfully.

I spent time in the off-season researching successful top bar beekeepers and what made their hives work for them. I also examined what it was that drew people to top bar hives. What I discovered was that the reasons for top-bar beekeeping revolved around several ideas. I have seen many traditional beekeepers just dismiss them offhand with the comment that they are just for "alternative" or hobby beekeepers and aren't practical. Well, I could see their points, too. So I made a list of pros and cons:

Pros:
- The beekeeper never has to lift more than one comb at a time.
- The bees make natural comb, eliminating the concern of hive contamination from wax foundation.
- It requires less manipulation by the beekeeper (assuming the hive is large enough) because there is room for expansion without the beekeeper adding new boxes.
- The horizontal configuration allows for the bees to naturally separate honey from brood without a queen excluder.
- It can be placed at waist level eliminating bending over by the beekeeper.

Cons:

- Since the comb is only attached by the top bar it is very fragile and can rip off if the beekeeper is not careful or twists the bar.
- The combs are not interchangeable between hives.
- The combs cannot be extracted.
- There is no inner cover and the bars are flush to one another so the hive must be disrupted quite a lot to do an inspection.
- The combs are often attached to the sides of the hive and need to be loosened prior to inspection (more disruption).
- The combs often get crooked or attached to one another (cross-combing)
- The beekeeper must start with a package or swarm because a traditional nucleus hive (nuc) or even a nuc from other top bar made to different dimensions cannot be installed in the hive.
- Many of the pre-made hives are not large enough and the hives are prone to swarming.
- Many of the pre-made hives do not have adequate ventilation, leading to mold and too much moisture in winter.
- Some are poorly designed and have the entrances in the middle of the hive.

I also observed that most top bar hives have an observation window. To me, that was neither here nor there because observation windows are not something that necessarily affects the success of the hive. After making this list and doing more research, a new thought entered my mind. For over 100 years people have used a horizontal frame hive. It is documented as far back as the 1860's. It is based on the traditional horizontal hives ancient civilizations used, but with frames. Using an article

Long hive in the experimental apiary

from a 1920 *Gleanings in Bee Culture* and ideas I found on the internet, I developed a plan for a Long Langstroth hive with frames – but foundationless frames - so we could get the natural comb. This solved the cons from the top bar list, but kept the pros. Even the need for the window was eliminated because regular self-spacing frames allow the beekeeper to look in without disturbing the bees. It doesn't work quite as well as an observation window, and I am sure one could be added to a horizontal frame hive, but I really have never felt the need for it.

I called up a fellow beekeeper who was also a woodworker. I asked him if he ever made his own equipment. When he said yes, I

launched into my crazy idea. Trust me, he thought I was crazy. I think he stills does, but he made the hive for me anyway. I asked him to make a box four feet long – the length of three Langstroth deep supers placed side by side. The entrance must be on one end because the bees will always place the

Self-spacing frames in a long Langstroth hive

brood in the front by the entrance and the honey in the back. If you put an entrance on the side, they will split the brood nest and more importantly, the honey. When winter comes, they will travel only one direction, and will run out of stores, being unable to get to the honey on the other side. On that note – yes, bees will travel horizontally. That is another objection, of course. I was told over and over that bees can only travel up in the winter, so if there aren't supers above, they will starve. Apparently the bees weren't aware of that, because they have overwintered very nicely moving from the front to the back of the hive. We chose the dimensions of deeps because they do need the combs to be a certain volume for overwintering, and mediums are just too shallow. Our entrance is on the broad side on one end. This is too large for the bees to defend, so we reduced it. I will detail the changes we made over time in a minute, but let me finish with the beginning.

My friend built the body of the hive and our first prototype had an unattached bottom board, just like a traditional hive, only three times as long. He put in the rabbets on the edges for the frames to hang on. I called a meeting of any local bee-keepers interested in top bar beekeeping. On a cool day in March, twenty-some bee-keepers gathered in my living room and looked at my "cof-fin" hive sitting in the middle of my living room. Some had been keeping bees in top bar hives for a period of time,

Mostly filled foundationless frame from long hive

some were interested, but hadn't done it yet. One had won a free top bar hive in a drawing and wanted more information so he could make it successful. We took turns discussing the pros and cons of top bar beekeeping, then I showed them my plan for the horizontal Langstroth hive. Some had never kept bees in a traditional hive and immediately saw the advantages of the self-spacing frames and the ability to transfer back and forth from traditional equipment. Top bar beekeepers always have to deal with how to keep comb straight, so they weren't as concerned with that. With the research I had done, I discovered that the key was leveling the hive. The bees will build their comb plumb-- straight from sky to ground-- so if the hive is level, the comb will be straight. They will also build the comb in line with previous comb and any little bit of crookedness will be ex-aggerated more and more as the comb goes back. Everyone left the meeting feeling like we had learned a lot, and most were convinced this design could be an answer to many of the problems the top bar solved, but could also solve many of its problems.

In May of that year, we placed the hive in our experimental apiary. We leveled it and put two frames of drawn comb in for a comb guide, just to give them a chance of keeping it straight. We put a foundationless frame in first by the entrance, then the two drawn frames, then filled the box –which holds 33 deep Langstroth frames (without propolis!) – with empty foundationless frames. We installed a package. We were faced with two problems from the outset – how to feed sugar water, and how to introduce the queen. The queen was in a California shipping cage, not an introduction cage. We decided the package had been together for long enough we would take the chance and directly introduce her. As far as the sugar water, we could have used a division board feeder, but we didn't have one, and the dandelions were in full bloom, so we took a big chance and didn't feed at all. It was an experimental apiary after all, right? Well, it

My double-walled long hive in my own apiary

worked, and worked beautifully. In just nine days they had completed five frames and the queen was happily laying. The year went perfectly, until sometime in the fall, when we discovered the hive being completely robbed out. I realized we had lost the queen somewhere along the line. Looking back, I think we were so excited about this new idea that during field days we were passing the frames (foundationless frames full of brood and honey) around a crowd of beekeepers. I think one of those times, poor queenie must have been lost without us realizing it. I learned to be a little more careful during hive inspections. With a traditional hive I always place the top cover upside down and put the first box on that, at an angle, so if the queen is there, she will drop into the cover, not into the grass. Of course I didn't have boxes to remove with the horizontal hive, and hadn't thought about those precautions! Over the winter we thought about what could improve the hive. The bees did great in the design. They produced plenty of honey. They ended up filling up 2/3 of the hive completely full before going queenless. That is the equivalent of two deeps. So, other than being more careful in the management, we thought about what could make it better for both beekeeper and bees. By this time, my son was getting into wood-working and was up to trying his hand at making me a hive. By spring we had it made. I had him double wall it and stuff the walls with wood shavings. We put a hinged lid on for the ease of the beekeeper. We just put a piece of sheet metal on the top, which hung over a bit to make an overhanging roof. He made an attached bottom board with a porch for the bees to alight on. We also made it ¾ of an inch longer so we could use three purchased inner covers rather than hav-ing to make custom inner covers. I had picked up a shipment of pack-age bees and the beekeepers were picking them up in my garage, so I could display our new hive for all of them to see when they came. Some were skeptical, but many thought it might be something worth trying themselves. I put that hive in my personal apiary. I bought a nucleus hive (nuc) from a beekeeper even farther north than me. These were Carniolans with a New World Carniolan queen. I popped the frames in my new hive just like I would have in a traditional deep box. I filled the rest of the hive with foundationless frames and away we went. The three inner covers were recessed in this hive, which was a little inconvenient, especially after they got propolized. Oth-erwise, this hive also did terrific. The bees overwintered just fine and took off the next spring. I was able to make splits off that hive, just by removing frames –again, the advantage of using traditional Lang-stroth deep frames. We re-populated the hive in the experimental apiary that spring with another package. We re-used all that drawn comb from the previous year. They did terrific as well and overwin-tered the coldest February on record with a leaky roof! We did have a blanket in the hive to absorb moisture that winter. We replaced the roof with a better one that summer.

The advantages of the Long Langstroth hive are:

- The beekeeper never has to lift more than one frame at a time, which gives access to those with less strength or even those with mobility problems.
- The hive has plenty of room for expansion, so the beekeeper doesn't have to worry about constant hive manipulations or swarming in the spring/early summer.
- The hinged lid means it can be lifted by one person, even if that person is not physically strong.
- The hive can be placed at a convenient height for the bee-keeper.
- Being off the ground, the entrance is not blocked by snow, even the year we had three feet on the ground in the apiary.
- The use of traditional frames gives the advantage of being able to transfer comb/brood/honey to and from traditional deeps.

The disadvantages:

- You can't move the hive very easily. When it is empty it weighs over 70 pounds, full – wow, let's just say it took four of us much effort to move it over one foot!
- Because of the first point, if you want to make a split, you have to move the brood out and can't leave the split on that location to receive foragers.
- The frames are all deeps, so now I have to keep deeps around for transfers and nucleus hives instead of using all mediums.
- The deep frames are harder to extract, especially the founda-tionless ones because of the weight.

So, the conclusion of the matter is that this is a great alternative for those who want to save their backs, or who are not physically able to handle heavy hive equipment. It is also good for the lazy/busy bee-keeper who can't get in the hive as often as he/she should. I have both designs and will continue to have both. I must admit, however, that during routine inspections, that horizontal hive is so easy to manage, it almost seems like cheating. If I get cross-combing, I adjust the level. That complicates things a little, but is not different than using the foundationless frames with traditional hives. You can run these horizontal hives with foundation. That makes it even easier. The day we moved the hive was a correction of the leveling. Rather than try to lift and shove shims in, we prepared a new pad/stand next to the hive, got it completely level, then moved the hive over to the new stand. That was just correcting one of our previous errors. Now we know how to prepare the site ahead of placing the hive to make it much easier to keep level.

Our current design which is still in the exper-imental stage is single walled, has a hinged lid and a chain to keep the lid open. We replaced our flat roof with a low-pitched peaked roof that over hangs to shed water. We covered the roof with rolled roofing material designed for flat roofs. It is self-adhe-sive and made of traditional asphalt roofing material. The hive has a solid, attached bottom board. We cut the entrance to be only 8

intermediate design long hive in progress

inches and put a porch roof over it to keep snow and ice off. We made a hive for another beekeeper who placed year-round foam in-sulation on it. This seemed to mess up the ventilation and it got too wet inside. We wanted to correct this and make it work, so we took off the foam insulation and re-worked the hive. The beekeeper really wanted it double walled, so we made it that way with the wood shav-ings inside for insulation because they breathe. We also made a peaked roof for her. The nice thing is that the bees seemed to thrive, even during experiments to make the hive better all summer long. With the single-walled hives, I insulate them exactly the same way as the traditional hives to prepare for winter. I think that is better than year-round insulation. They need the breathing and additional ventilation in the summer, although my double-walled hive with wood shavings does not collect excess moisture. The wood shavings do attract carpenter ants, though. We tried putting cedar chips in the double walled hive made for the other beekeeper. Our thought was it might deter the ants, but we are not sure if that is true or not.

Chapter 14
The Conclusion of the Matter

In the end, the decision is up to each individual beekeeper if he or she is willing to "think outside the box" and try some new ideas to save beekeeping. Notice I did not say, "save the bees". This is because if we beekeepers fail, the bees will just move to feral locations and live happily, probably more happily, without us! If we want to keep getting honey and stop the depressing cycle of all our bees dying every year and replacing them with more bees that will die again, we have to make some fundamental changes. Production livestock agriculture has its problems, but the livestock can live (probably shorter lives) and produce under very stressful and unnatural circumstances. They are often pressed and bred to produce way more than is natural for them. They do it, at a cost to their health, but they do it. Because bees are wild animals, they simply won't. They will just die or abscond. They will absolutely not be pushed beyond their biological limits. Livestock producers discovered that most breeds of animals are actually that way. That is why almost all production dairy cows are Holsteins and most meat chickens and pigs are all one breed. Those breeds could handle the unnatural situations and the unreasonable production demands without dying immediately.

As beekeepers we need to revise some of our thinking in terms of production as well. If the locally adapted bee that overwinters well makes a little less honey, we have to accept that. Maybe the super-bee that is adapted to tropical climates produces way more honey, but they all die in the winter. Now we have to start fresh with new bees again. Some people actually do that as a management style. They got so tired of fighting the overwintering battle, they gave up. They collect every drop of honey, let the bees die and buy new bees in the spring. Alternately, some sell the bees in the fall to pollinators going south, and still start fresh in the spring. That is an option, but if you want to see beekeeping continue over the long haul, that is not the best solution. Any good solution will require some give and take on both sides of the equation. So, if we give the bees more latitude to be what they are supposed to be, they will reward us with honey and survival.

My personal techniques are just what I have adapted for my own use. I am constantly evaluating and revising my management and hive designs. I will continue to do that until I don't keep bees any more. Hopefully that will be the day I die. If I make beekeeping simple enough for myself, why not? I did read about a 102 year old beekeeper and he was keeping bees in a traditional hive. With my "cheater" horizontal hive, surely I could hobble out there and check on my ladies, don't you think? I want beekeeping to not just continue, but to thrive and be accessible to anyone who has the desire and discipline to do it. I don't want it to be killed by people who are unwilling to let go of ideas and techniques that obviously are no longer working. I want beekeepers not only to use their brains to evaluate, but to be willing to make the changes necessary to preserve this fascinating art and hobby for many generations to come.

I recently read some articles published by beekeepers in 2007, right at the point that "CCD" appeared. At that time, many were actually trying (and many succeeding) to keep bees without chemical controls. A mere eight years later the same people were completely unwilling to admit that it could ever be possible to keep bees without chemical controls. I don't know if it is just giving up, or if they have a collective amnesia to the very things they were doing less than a decade ago. I understand that some are keeping bees in very difficult circumstances, like regions prone to severe droughts. I can't tell them what to do or how to run their businesses. I just wonder how they can ever make a profit under those circumstances. I don't keep bees to make money. I think that is why I have a measure of success. I don't have the pressure of needing my bees to produce to make my livelihood. Many beekeepers in the past expressed the opinion that commercial beekeepers should stick to honey production because pollination brings too many risks and stresses. It is hard to make honey in arid regions. I don't have an answer for that. Perhaps it isn't appropriate to keep bees in places where there are only a few naturally blooming plants and those have naturally adapted pollina-tors that come out at night, when bees are in their hives.

Many people have expressed the thought that bees are like the "ca-nary in the mine" that are the first indicators of an environment that is getting unhealthy. I disagree with that. Bees and beekeepers have always trailed at the back of the agricultural trends. I think they are just an end-game indicator of what is wrong with our commercial ag-riculture system. Scientists think that living things can be produced like products in a factory. They have developed an input-output sys-tem that they would like to produce consistent, high quality results. They feel as though if they put in input A + input B they will get output C. The problem is that living things are too complex and their eco-systems are equally complex. There are too many uncontrolled (and uncontrollable) variables. They deal with that by putting the animals or plants in more controlled situations – highly concentrated housing for animals or hydroponics for plants. This does help give them a more consistent and controlled output – of food shaped objects. Like I stated before, some specially bred breeds of plants and animals can tolerate this for a short time and produce a product that looks like real food. But it is very intensive in its requirements and the inputs must always happen on schedule. It is very dependent on the trans-portation system and food requirements and every part of the sys-tem being in place at the right time. When this is attempted with bees, it stresses them to their breaking point, and they simply die or go away. It sounds a little like CCD, doesn't it? The bees just illustrate more graphically what is going on in the entire industrialized agricul-ture system. The good news is that not all people keep bees like that, and not all people keep livestock and grow plants that way, either.

The more of us who decide to work with nature instead of against it, the better the bees and the rest of the natural world will be for it. If each person just takes the initiative to do it in their own little world, it eventually adds up. This makes for a healthy bee population and eventually it will begin to have a ripple effect backward. When enough of us small beekeepers begin to demonstrate the success of the system that grows better, stronger bees, eventually those involved in industrialized agriculture will have to sit up and take notice. Especially if we are the only people left who have healthy bees! So, I say if you are tired of fighting the same old, depressing cycle of failure and dead bees, try it. What do you have to lose? If you are losing a large number of bees anyway, what can it hurt to try a different approach? The reward can be very sweet indeed!

References/Resources

Abbott Farms website: www.abbottsustainablefarms.com

American Bee Journal, 51 S. 2nd St., Hamilton, IL 62341, www.americanbeejournal.com

Bush, Michael. *The Practical Beekeeper*. X-Star Publishing, 2004- 2011.

Dadant, C.P. *First Lessons in Beekeeping*. Illinois: Dadant and Sons. 1976 edition.

Disselkoen, Mel. *OTS Queen Rearing*. Wyoming, MI: International Mating Nuc, Inc. 2014.

Dolittle, G.M. *Scientific Queen Rearing*. Hebden Bridge, UK: Northern Bee Books 2010, re-print of original 1901 manuscript published by George W. York & Company, Chicago, IL.

Dolittle, G.M. *A Year's Work in An Out-Apiary*. Hebden Bridge, UK: Northern Bee Books 2013, re-print of original 1910 manuscript published by A.I. Root Co. Medina, OH.

Langstroth, L.L. *Langstroth's Hive and the Honey-bee*. Mineola, NY: Dover Publications, Inc. 2004, re-print of original manuscript published in 1878 by J.B. Lippincott & Co. Philadelphia, under the title *A Practical Treatise on the Hive and Honey-Bee*.

Mangum, Wyatt A. Ph.D. *Top-Bar Hive Beekeeping: Wisdom and Pleasure Combined*. Bowling Green, VA: Stinging Drone Publications, 2012.

Miller, C.C. *Fifty Years Among the Bees*. New York: Dover Publications, Inc. 2006, re-print of original 1915 manuscript published by A.I. Root Co. Medina, OH.

Pellet, Frank C. *History of American Beekeeping*. Ames, IA: Collegiate Press, Inc. 1938. Re-printed by Wicwas Press, Kalamazoo, MI, 2013.

Root, E.R. "Long Idea Hive Again". *Gleanings in Bee Culture* May 1920: 268-271.

Root Publishing. *The ABC & XYZ of Bee Culture – 40th Edition*. Medina, OH: A.I. Root Co., 1990.

Taylor, Richard. *The Joys of Beekeeping*. Interlaken, NY: Linden Books, 1984.

Acknowledgments

I would like to express my deep appreciation to the individuals and publishing companies that have re-printed the historic works that are cited here. Without those re-prints it is very difficult to get the valuable information contained in these texts. Originals of these works are 100 or more years old and are rare and often fragile if they can be obtained at all in print form. Some of the more contemporary texts have been updated, such as *ABC & XYZ of Bee Culture* and *First Lessons in Beekeeping*, but these updates often reflect the very prejudices I am trying to dispel, so I recommend the older versions. The varroa mite entered the American beekeeping scene in the late 1980's and early 1990's depending on the region. Books written prior to that time have more level-headed beekeeping information in my opinion than those written later. However, literature written prior to 2006 has a lot of good information in it as well. After 2006 and the advent of "CCD", desperation set in and most of what has been published or updated since has been heavily skewed toward chemical controls. I personally like to have hard, print copies of books, so I am grateful for the publishers that have recognized the value of historic books and have made them available to the general public in print form.